The Montessori School of the Angels, Inc.

The Collegeville
ATLAS
of the
BIBLE

The Collegeville
ATLAS
of the BIBLE

A Liturgical Press Book

THE LITURGICAL PRESS
Collegeville, Minnesota

The Collegeville Atlas of the Bible
was conceived, edited and designed by
Team Media Limited
Masters House
107 Hammersmith Road
London W14 0QH

© Team Media Limited 1998

This book is published in the United States of America and Canada by The Liturgical Press, Collegeville, Minnesota 56321.

Printed in Italy by Officine Grafiche DeAgostini.

1   2   3   4   5   6   7   8   9

Library of Congress Cataloging-in-Publication Data

Harpur, James.
    The Collegeville atlas of the Bible / Jay Harpur and Marcus Braybrooke.
       p.   cm.
    Includes bibliographical references.
    ISBN 0-8146-2702-1 (alk. paper)
    1. Bible—History of Biblical events.   2. Bible—History of contemporary events.   3. Bible—Geography—Maps.   4. Bible—Geography.   I. Braybrooke, Marcus.   II. Title.
BS635.2H38   1999
220.9'5—dc21
                              99-18653
                              CIP

Bible Atlas Team:

Project Editors:
Simon Adams
Julia Bruce
David Scott-Macnab

Editors:
David Girling
Simon Hall
Nicholas Jones
Fiona Plowman

Art Editors:
Thomas Keenes
Malcolm Smythe

Assistant Designer:
Duncan Paré

Editorial research:
Fiona Plowman

Picture research:
Veneta Bullen

Cartographers:
Oxford Cartographers

Illustrator:
Roger Hutchins

Team Media
Editorial Director: Louise Tucker
Managing Editor: Elizabeth Tatham
Art Directors: Eddie Poulton,
Paul Wilkinson

Old Testament Author:
Marcus Braybrooke

New Testament Author:
James Harpur

Consultants:
Marcus Braybrooke
Felicity Cobbing

Marcus Braybrooke is a Church of England vicar and also Co-president of the World Congress of Faiths. He has written several books about the Bible, Judaism, and interfaith relations. His books include *Faith in a Global Age, How to Understand Judaism* and *Wisdom of Jesus.*

Felicity Cobbing works at the Palestine Exploration Fund and specializes in the Archaeology of the Ancient Levant. She excavates in Jordan and has written a number of academic and popular articles. She has acted as a consultant on several books on the Ancient Mediterranean.

James Harpur has written and edited several books on religion and the Bible, including *The Atlas of Sacred Places, Great Events of Bible Times* and *The Journeys of St. Paul.* His interest in the sacred is also shown in two volumes of poetry.

Contents

Stone relief of the Ark of the Covenant from Capernaum

From Genesis to Revelation, the Bible contains over 50 books (the exact number varies between versions), which are divided into the Old and New Testaments. The Old Testament describes the striving of the Jewish people to find and keep a homeland, and it details their covenants, or agreements, with God. The New Testament records the life and death of Jesus Christ, whose followers believed that he was Israel's long-awaited savior, or Messiah; it then goes on to relate the spread of Christ's teachings by Paul and other apostles of the early Christian Church.

The Bible does not, however, present a straightforward historical account of the founding of Israel and its subsequent

■ But the land that you are crossing over to occupy is a land of hills and valleys, watered by rain from the sky, a land that the Lord your God looks after.

Deuteronomy 11:11

fortunes; nor does it set out a methodical biography of Jesus. Both testaments present a variety of material, some of it historical, some prophetic or poetic, and some that has a mythic or legendary flavor. Whatever the nature of these narratives, they are all located in or around the land known since the 5th century BCE as 'Palestine.' This area is also variously referred to – in whole or part – as the Holy Land, the Promised Land, Canaan, Judea – or Judah – and Israel.

The Promised Land is first referred to in Genesis, when Abraham is called by God to leave his home in Mesopotamia and seek out Canaan, a country promised to him and his children by God. In return, God demands that Abraham and his descendants renounce forever the worship of other gods.

Abraham's faith and acceptance of these terms established the first covenant between the Jewish people and the Lord.

Exodus recounts how Abraham's descendants, the Israelites, escaped from servitude in Egypt. Under the leadership of Moses they endured an arduous journey through the desert to reach Canaan. It was here that the first kings – Saul, David and Solomon – created the Kingdom of Israel. This land remained of fundamental importance to its people throughout its subsequent history – its division into the rival kingdoms of Israel and Judah, their fall to the Assyrians and Babylonians, the exile of the people of Judah, and their return to a land ruled in turn by Persia, Greece, and Rome.

In New Testament times, the Holy Land forms the backdrop to Jesus' short but dynamic life, during which he taught Jews and Gentiles alike that a new way of life was possible through the love of God.

History and the land

Any understanding of the Bible should begin, therefore, with an appreciation of the land in which its dramas were played out, together with an understanding of the political geography of the ancient Near East. Palestine lay directly between the great powers of Egypt in the southwest and Mesopotamia in the northeast and, over time, was frequently invaded by both.

Within the Holy Land itself, the Israelites had to contend with the hostility of the indigenous peoples who resented their presence. Furthermore, groups of exiles with pagan beliefs who had settled in Canaan from Assyria and Babylon, presented a constant challenge to the Jewish faith.

**Left: Gold plaque from Canaan showing Egyptian influence.
Above: Moses strikes water from a rock in the desert.
Right: View of the land of Canaan.**

The River Jordan winds its way south from the Sea of Galilee.

The city of Jerusalem, holy to Jews, Christians, and Muslims.

The biblical Holy Land was relatively small – about 240km (150 miles) in length from the traditional landmarks of Dan in the north to Beersheba in the south. Its width, from the Jordan Valley in the east to the Mediterranean Sea in the west, varied between 50 and 130km (30–80 miles). Despite its size, this compact area was diverse in climate and landscape.

The most productive region was the coastal plain, which stretched north to the great Phoenician trading cities of Tyre and Sidon. Toward the south lay the land of the Philistines, whose conflict with Israel is epitomized in the epic combat between the young David and the Philistine champion Goliath. Inland, on a plateau dominating the north of the Holy Land, lay Galilee, a fertile area of orchards and olive groves where Jesus lived and taught. The heart of the region was the Sea of Galilee itself – a large freshwater lake, where Jesus recruited his first disciples. It lies about 215m (700 feet) below sea level in the Great Rift Valley that runs from eastern

Turkey to Africa. From it flows the River Jordan, which Joshua and the Israelites crossed to enter the Promised Land, and in whose waters Jesus was baptized by John the Baptist.

Bordered by steep cliffs, the Jordan runs south to the Dead Sea, nearly 400m (1300 feet) below sea level. It was in caves at Qumran, in the hills above the Dead Sea, that ancient biblical texts known as the Dead Sea Scrolls were found. Close to the sea's western shore stands the palace-fortress of Masada, where Jewish Zealots committed mass suicide in 73 CE after the failure of the Jewish rebellion against Rome.

About 24km (15 miles) west of the Dead Sea's northern shore stands Jerusalem – the city that became the capital of King David, was destroyed by the Babylonians, rebuilt and beautified by Herod the Great, and razed by the Romans in 70 CE. Here, in the spiritual center of Judaism, stood the Temple – the holiest place of the Jews – which once housed the Ark of the Covenant, Israel's most sacred relic that contained the Ten Commandments given to Moses. Here, too, are the landmarks associated with the last days of Jesus, including Gethsemane and the Via Dolorosa – the traditional route to the site of Jesus' execution.

Journeys and maps

The topography of the Bible lands is therefore central to this book. So also are the shifting political boundaries of the Middle East during biblical times and the epic journeys taken by individuals as well as nations, which play such a prominent part in the Old Testament. In the books of the New Testament, the journeys of Jesus are on a smaller scale, but the missions of St Paul to take Christianity to Asia Minor and Europe are heroic in their scope.

Using photographs, maps, and groundplans, and taking into account recent archeological research, the following pages retell the major stories of the Bible in the context of their time and place. Reconstructions of cities and buildings help to bring the biblical world to life and so to shed further light on the stories that lie at the heart of the great religions of Judaism and Christianity.

St Paul

Nineteenth-century Torah scroll from Iraq

The central concern of the Old Testament is the unique relationship between God and the Jews – the nation of Israel. This relationship, the Jews believe, was founded on a covenant made between God and the 'patriarchs' – their first great ancestors, including Abraham and Jacob. God promised that in return for their loyalty and obedience, he would make their descendants a great nation and give them Canaan, the 'Promised Land.'

The theme of this special relationship pervades the Old Testament – or Tanach in Judaism – but the scope of its books extends far beyond this. They include the divine laws of the first five books of the Bible, also known as the Pentateuch or Torah; historical works; prophecies; psalms; philosophical discussions; proverbs and wise sayings. Each book has found its way into the biblical canon – or official scriptures – because it helped to reveal the character and purpose of God.

Christian versions of the Old Testament differ in the number and order of books included. Some Jewish books, such as the First and Second Books of the Maccabees, are not found in the official Hebrew scriptures, but first appeared in the 3rd century BCE in the Greek version of the Old Testament known as the Septuagint. They were also included in the Vulgate Bible – the Latin translation of the late 4th century CE used by the Catholic Church. Catholic versions of the Bible still include these books; Protestant versions omit them or put them in an appendix, known as the Apocrypha.

The Old Testament and history

Although the Old Testament presents its stories as historical events, modern scholars are still trying to separate fact from myth and legend in their content. Various episodes of the first

3000BCE	2500	2000	1500	1250	1000	900	800

Old Testament events

The dates of biblical events in this chronology are only approximate. Dates for Egypt are taken from the Low Chronology which is currently the most widely accepted view.

● *Exodus (between c.1279–1213)*

Saul's reign (1030–1000)

● *Conquest of Canaan by the Israelites (c.1200)*

David's reign (1000–960)

Solomon's reign (960–931)

● *Building of first Temple c.956*

● *Philistines settle in eastern Mediterranean (c.1200)*

● *Kingdom divides into Judah and Israel (930)*

Fertility goddess figure from the Philistine temple at Tell Qasile

Ivory pomegranate carving from the Solomonic period

Empires and their rulers

Mesopotamian man leading a goat, on a mosaic from Ur

Old Babylonian Period (1792–1595)

King Hammurabi (1792–1750)

Middle Assyrian Empire (1750–1000)

Hittite Empire (c.1400–1180)

Neo-Assyrian Empire (c.1000–609)

1st Intermediate Period

2nd Intermediate Period

Egypt

Old Kingdom (2700–2190)

Middle Kingdom (2040–1759)

New Kingdom (1530–1100)

Thutmose III (1479–1425)

Tutankhamun (1336–1327)

Winged sphinx in ivory from Assyria

● *Hyksos take control of Egypt (c.1674)*

Rameses II (1279–1213)

● *Thutmose III begins to build his empire in Palestine (c.1457)*

● *Sheshonq I's campaigns in Palestine (c.925–924)*

11 chapters of Genesis, in particular, have a mythic flavor. The story of Noah and the flood, for example, is similar to flood stories in other Middle Eastern cultures. Even so, the lack of direct evidence for characters such as Noah does not prove they did not exist. They may have been real people to whom heroic legendary deeds were later attributed.

Reliable historical evidence is scant for the period of the patriarchs, who may have lived up to 4000 years ago. Some time later, events pertaining to the Jewish nation begin to figure in the records of other civilizations. An Assyrian obelisk, for instance, refers to Jehu's seizure of power in Israel in 841 BCE, while the siege of the Judean city of Lachish in 701 BCE is depicted in Assyrian reliefs; both events feature in the Second Book of Kings. Many other figures and events of the Bible are mentioned by the records of other great civilizations, including the Egyptians, Greeks, and Romans.

Historical and archeological evidence undoubtedly illuminates, and sometimes supports, biblical texts. The story of the Tower of Babel, for instance, may have been inspired by the great stepped towers, or ziggurats, of Mesopotamia. Equally, archeological investigations can contradict or throw doubt on events and dates as reported in the Bible. The excavations at Jericho, for example, have failed to corroborate details of the biblical account of the city's fall to the Israelites.

Another topic of debate is the authorship of the Old Testament. Some parts have been attributed to figures such as Moses, but modern scholars think that the stories began as oral accounts and short texts gathered from various sources, which were later compiled into books. Different stylistic strands and various textual discrepancies support this theory.

Such scholarly discussion and analysis about the historical validity and cultural context of the Old Testament should not, however, obscure the fact that for Jews, Christians, and Muslims its books are timeless sacred texts, whose reflections on the great mysteries of life, death and destiny are still as relevant today as they were when they were first composed.

700	600	500	400	300	200	100	50

• *The Assyrians conquer Israel (722)*

•*Judah becomes vassal of Nebuchadnezzar (605)*

• *Nehemiah rebuilds the walls of Jerusalem (445)*

• *Antiochus IV desecrates the Temple in Jerusalem (169)*

• *Judah falls to the Babylonians (586)*

Maccabean campaigns (166–60)

• *Lachish attacked by Sennacherib (701)*

The Israelites return to Judah (537–445)

• *Judean independence from Seleucid Empire (142)*

Temple in Jerusalem rebuilt (536–519)

Dragon figure from the Ishtar Gate in the ancient city of Babylon

Nebuchadnezzar (605–562)

Neo-Babylonian Period (587/6–539)

• *Fall of Babylon (539)*

Scythian gold bracelet

Persian Empire (549–331)

Tiglath-pileser III (745–727)

Cyrus the Great (549–530)

Shalmaneser V (727–722)

Darius I (522–486)

• *Alexander the Great destroys the Persian Empire (332)*

Terracotta figure of a Seleucid war elephant from Asia Minor

Sargon II (722–705)

Xerxes (486–465)

Hellenistic Period (334–30)

Sennacherib (705–681)

Artaxerxes I (465–424)

Seleucid Dynasty, Syria (305–84/3)

Rome founded (753)

• *The Roman Republic begins (509)*

3rd Intermediate Period   Late Dynastic Period (661–332)

Ptolemaic Dynasty (305–51)

Neco II (610–595)

Ptolemy I (305–282)

• *Egypt falls to the Persians (525)*

Adam and Eve in the Garden of Eden

The Bible begins with the story of the creation of the universe by God, the single, all-powerful creator. It was the Jews' belief in one God that marked them apart from their Mesopotamian neighbors, who worshiped many gods and believed that the universe was the result of primeval battles between rival deities.

The Bible does not offer any explanations about the origins of life. Rather, it affirms that everything depended on God. The Bible then goes on to explain in various myths and legends how God's work became corrupt and how good and evil came to coexist in the world.

In one story of creation, God's first act was to make the heavens and the earth. He then declared, 'Let there be light,' and over six successive days he separated dry land from the oceans, made the sun, moon and stars, and created plants, fish and other living creatures. Finally, as the climax of his creative work, God created human beings in his own image.

■ In the beginning when God created the heavens and the earth, the earth was a form-less void and darkness covered the face of the deep, while a wind from God swept over the face of the waters. Genesis 1:1

In another account God made a beautiful fertile garden in Eden. He put the garden in the care of Adam and told him that he said could eat the fruit of every tree, except the tree of the knowledge of good and evil. Then God created Eve, as his companion.

The temptation of Eve
Unfortunately, human beings soon proved unworthy of God's trust. A serpent, so the story goes, approached Eve and tempted her to eat some forbidden fruit and then give some to Adam. Having eaten the fruit, Adam and Eve woke as if from the innocence of childhood and became aware of sin and evil. They became ashamed of their nakedness and sewed fig leaves together to cover their bodies. Then God came into the garden and asked who had told them they were naked. Adam blamed Eve, who blamed the serpent. In punishment, the serpent was condemned to crawl on its belly, the woman to endure the pain of childbirth, and the man to find food only by hard work. Adam and Eve were banished from Eden and sent out into the world to fend for themselves.

Adam and Eve had two sons – Cain, a farmer, and Abel, a shepherd. In time, they both offered gifts to God, but God rejected Cain's offering. Cain was so angry that he killed Abel, and in response God banished Cain to the land of Nod – that is, to become a nomad, or wanderer.

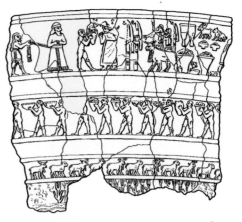

All the Mesopotamian peoples had myths to help them make sense of the creation of the world. Many of these involve warring gods. The alabaster Warka vase (left, detail above), dating from c.3000 BCE, comes from the temple treasury at Uruk. It depicts priests bringing offerings to Inanna, goddess of love and war – just one of the deities that the early Jews rejected when they turned toward a single God.

The Fertile Crescent
Home to some of the world's earliest civilizations, the Fertile Crescent stretched in an arc from the river valleys of the Tigris and Euphrates in the east, to the coastline of the Mediterranean in the west. The natural fertility of the land meant that it was one of the first areas in which people could plant crops and live in settled villages. By 4000 BCE, the first cities had been constructed, giving rise to all-powerful empires. The Jews, who trace their origins back to Abraham, were among the many peoples who lived in the Fertile Crescent.

EGYPT

Thebes

0   100   200 Kilometers
0   100   200 Miles

Although it is not possible to identify the imagined location of the Garden of Eden, the author of Genesis might well have been inspired by the green valleys of the rivers Euphrates (right) and Tigris. Lush vegetation grows along the banks of these rivers, providing havens for birds, animals, and people, and contrasting strongly with the emptiness of the surrounding desert.

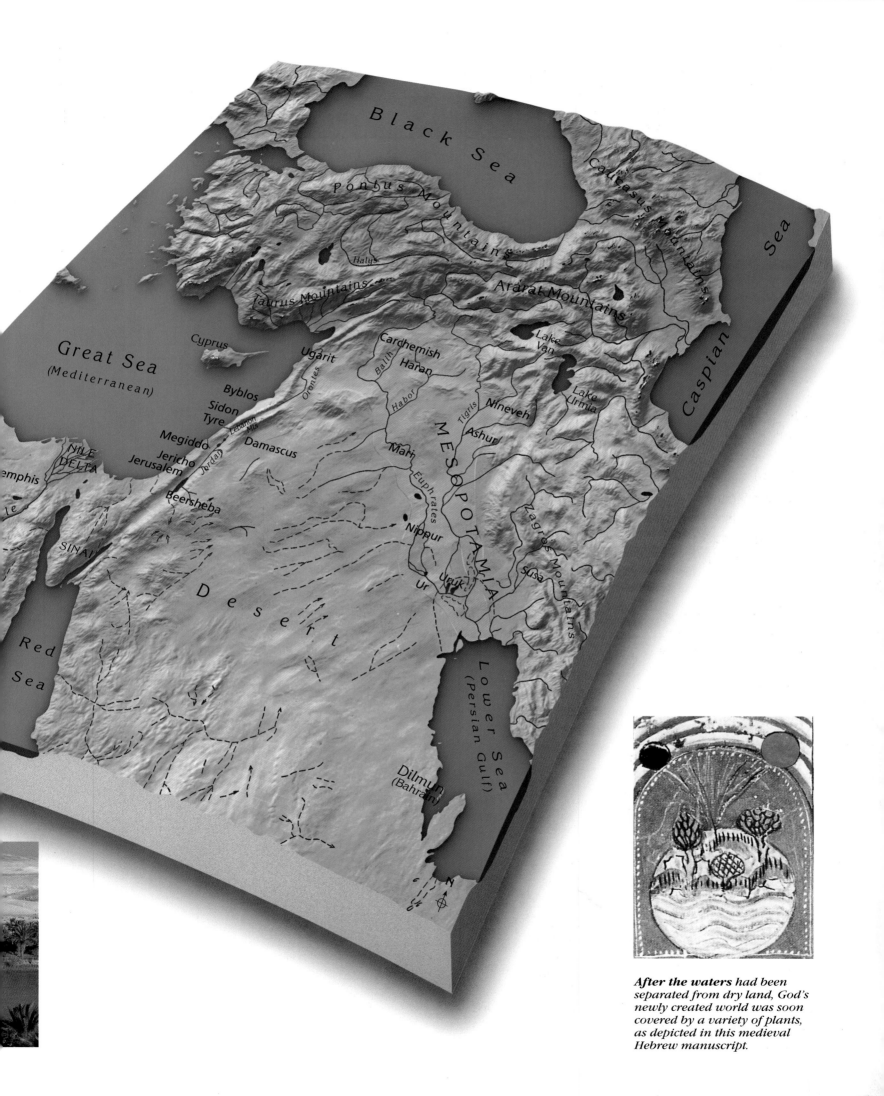

Black Sea

Caucasus Mountains

Pontus Mountains

Halys

Taurus Mountains

Ararat Mountains

Lake Van

Cyprus

Carchemish

Ugarit

Balih

Haran

Lake Urmia

Caspian Sea

Great Sea
(Mediterranean)

Byblos

Sidon
Tyre

Orontes

Habor

Tigris

Nineveh

Ashur

MESOPOTAMIA

Lebanon
Mts

Megiddo

Damascus

Mari

NILE
DELTA

Jericho

Jordan

Jerusalem

Euphrates

Memphis

Beersheba

Nippur

Zagros Mountains

Susa

Nile

SINAI

Uruk

Ur

Desert

Red

Sea

Lower
Sea
(Persian Gulf)

Dilmun
(Bahrain)

N

After the waters had been separated from dry land, God's newly created world was soon covered by a variety of plants, as depicted in this medieval Hebrew manuscript.

Noah's ark, from a late 13th-century Hebrew prayer book

In the generations that followed Cain and Abel the wickedness of the world increased to such a degree that God became sorry that he had ever created humankind at all. He was greatly saddened by all the violence and immorality of the world, and he decided that he would wipe human beings off the face of the earth, together with all other living creatures, in a single, massive flood. Only one man stood out as a beacon of righteousness in this world of sin, and his name was Noah. God decided that of all humanity he would save just Noah and his immediate family because Noah was the only blameless person in an otherwise corrupt generation.

Building the ark

God warned Noah that he was going to send a flood which would destroy all life on earth, and instructed him how to build an ark that would ensure safety for his family. God also told Noah to gather one pair of every kind of living creature

■ They went into the ark with Noah, two and two of all flesh in which there was the breath of life. And those that entered, male and female of all flesh, went in as God had commanded him; and the Lord shut him in.

Genesis 7:15–16

The Epic of Gilgamesh

The biblical account of Noah is not the only flood story from ancient Mesopotamia. In the 19th century, thousands of clay tablets from the library of the Assyrian king Ashurbanipal (668–627 BCE) were found at Nineveh, the Assyrian capital. Among them were ten (one at right) that record a long Babylonian poem called *The Epic of Gilgamesh*. The poem tells how the hero, Gilgamesh, sets out to discover the secret of everlasting life. His quest takes him to a man called Utnapishtim – the 'Noah' figure of the Babylonian story – who describes how he was the only man to survive a great flood, and in this way he achieved immortality. The account also relates how birds were sent out from his ship

and ends with a sacrifice to the gods. The epic is so vivid that it seems like an eyewitness account. Some scholars have suggested that it may describe a great tidal wave caused by a cyclone that swept up the alluvial plain of the rivers Euphrates and Tigris and flooded a large area of Mesopotamia.

Mount Ararat *in modern Turkey (above) may possibly be the mountain referred to in the biblical story of the flood. Early in the 19th century, a mountain shepherd claimed to have seen a great wooden ship* *on its summit. However, no archeological evidence of an ark has been found to substantiate either this, or similar claims at other suggested sites in the Zagros and Ararat mountain ranges.*

into the ark so that they too would be preserved. Noah duly constructed the ark from cypress wood. It was 150m (480 ft) long, 25m (75 ft) wide, and 15m (45 ft) high.

Seven days before the rain was due to begin, Noah took his family, consisting of his wife and their three sons and his sons' wives, and pairs of all the living creatures into the ark. The rain came pouring down and lasted for 40 days and 40 nights. It rained so fiercely that it was as if all the floodgates of the heavens had been opened. As the rain continued, the water began to rise, lifting the ark until it floated. The water became so deep that even the tops of mountains disappeared from view. Every living thing on earth died, except for Noah and the people and animals in the ark.

Noah sent out the dove for a third time, but on this occasion it did not return. Noah then knew that the surface of the earth was dry, and that it was at last safe to disembark.

After the flood

God told Noah to bring all the living creatures out of the ark, so that they might disperse and multiply. In gratitude for their deliverance from the terrible flood, Noah built an altar and made a sacrifice to God. This pleased God, and he blessed Noah and his family, urging him to be fruitful and increase in number. God also told Noah that henceforth all living creatures would fear human beings and that everything that lived and moved, fish, birds, and beasts of the earth, would provide them with food.

God was pleased with Noah and assured him that never again would he subject humanity to such a cataclysm. As an eternal reminder of this promise he said that, whenever people saw dark clouds gathering and feared another flood, he would send a rainbow to assure them of his resolve.

After Noah's sacrifice, God promised him that he would never again send a flood to destroy all living creatures. As a reminder of this, a rainbow would always appear among threatening storm clouds.

Noah ensured that a male and a female of every living creature, even of species as large and fearsome as those featured in this Roman mosaic hunting scene (below), would survive to repopulate the earth.

The rains cease

Finally, the rain abated and the flood waters gradually began to subside. One hundred and fifty days after the height of the flood, the waters receded and the ark came to rest on top of Mount Ararat. Noah sent out birds to assess how far the waters had dropped. First he sent a raven, but instead of flying back to the ark, it kept circling around until the land reappeared. Noah then sent out a dove, but, finding nowhere to land, it returned to the ark. Seven days later, Noah sent the dove out again and it came back with a freshly plucked olive leaf in its beak. This indicated to Noah that the trees had reappeared, but as the bird had still returned he realized that the land itself was still under water. After seven more days,

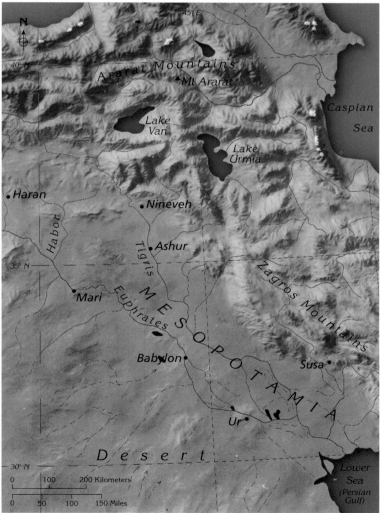

Mesopotamian flood plain

The two great rivers of Mesopotamia, the Tigris and the Euphrates, were subject to sudden floods that sometimes spread over huge areas, and could even make the rivers

themselves change direction. Like the Babylonian flood story in The Epic of Gilgamesh, *the Genesis account may have been inspired by one of these catastrophic events.*

Construction of the Tower of Babel

After the flood, the descendants of Noah's three sons – Shem, Ham, and Japheth – settled near the city of Ur in Sumer, or Shinar, as the Bible calls it, in southern Mesopotamia. According to the author of Genesis, the people of Shinar became so skilful and self-confident that they decided to build a city, called Babel, with a tower that would reach up to heaven. Yet, as the Bible humorously points out, the tower was so small in God's eyes that he had made the effort to come down from heaven to have a closer look for himself.

The story of the Tower of Babel was probably inspired by the great towers, known as ziggurats, built in Sumer from

> ■ Then they said, 'Come let us build ourselves a city, and a tower with its top in the heavens, and let us make a name for ourselves; otherwise we shall be scattered abroad upon the face of the whole earth.'
> Genesis 11:4

about 2100 BCE. The purpose of these amazing constructions is unclear, but scholars suggest that they represented a cosm mountain, a giant altar or a divine throne, where Sumerian kings – who were semidivine figures – held religious rites to ensure the welfare of their dominions.

According to the Bible, when God saw the tower, he was concerned, not that human beings might usurp his power, but that their moral development had not kept pace with their technological skill. God changed the language of the builders so that they were unable to understand each other. As a result, they could not finish the city and its tower, and they scattered across the world, all speaking different languages. The city, we are told, was called Babel – a deliberate pun on the Hebrew word meaning 'confused.'

The Bible goes on to tell how Terah, the father of Abram (later Abraham), lived near the city of Ur with his family. At some point after Abram had married, Terah decided to leave the region, taking his family north to the city of Haran (modern Harran in southeast Turkey).

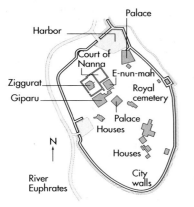

Ur was dominated by its great ziggurat, located in a sacred enclosure in the north of the city. The sacred precinct also contained the Court of Nanna, the E-nun-mah, which may have been a treasury, and the Giparu, or residence of the chief priestess. Buildings that have been identified elsewhere in the city include palaces, houses of ordinary people, and a royal cemetery. Ur was protected by walls and a moat fed from the River Euphrates.

Palace
Harbor
Court of Nanna
E-nun-mah
Ziggurat
Giparu
Royal cemetery
Palace
Houses
N
Houses
River Euphrates
City walls

The royal cemetery of Ur has yielded many beautiful objects, including this magnificent ram (left), with gold legs and a body of lapis lazuli. Its presence in a tomb is seen as evidence of a belief in the afterlife.

The Ziggurat of Ur
King Ur-Nammu built the mighty ziggurat of Ur in about 2100 BCE. It is typical of many similar structures erected in ancient Mesopotamia. Three platforms of diminishing size rose one above the other. At the top stood a temple in the form of a tower. The base of the ziggurat, which survives largely intact, covers some 2290m² (24,650 sq ft).

Builders in ancient Sumer used bricks that were made from straw and clay, then fired in a kiln or left to dry in the sun – methods still used by brickmakers in the area today.

The ziggurats were impressive buildings by any standard, requiring great skills in both planning and construction. This seal (left) shows Babylonian builders at work.

The temple at the top was dedicated to Nanna, the moon god and patron of the city of Ur

Ziggurat Sites
Ziggurats were built over a wide area of Mesopotamia. Red dots on the map indicate major ziggurat sites. The map also shows the distribution of the main peoples of the region at about 2100 BCE.

The walls slope inward at the top, following a convex curve, which makes the building appear more graceful

The outer walls were faced with fired brick and reinforced with buttresses; behind these walls, each platform was completely solid

Abraham's Journey

Mesopotamian man leading a goat

Abraham, a descendant of Noah, was living near the city of Haran in Mesopotamia, when God instructed him to turn his back on his own gods, leave his country, and go to Canaan. In return, God promised Abraham, then known as Abram, that his family would one day be a great nation blessed by God.

Abraham took his wife Sarah, his nephew Lot, his servants, and his flocks of sheep and goats. On arriving in Canaan, they settled in the semidesert area known as the Negeb, but were driven farther south to Egypt by famine.

It was in Egypt that Abraham became a wealthy man. Using what was probably a traditional legend, the Bibel tells that Abraham feared Sarah's great beauty would inflame the Egyptians to desire her, and kill him to have her. He therefore told Sarah to say she was his sister, not his wife. The Pharaoh therefore took her as his wife. Angered by this, God inflicted disease upon the Pharoah who, discovering that Sarah was

■ I will make of you a great nation, and I will bless you, and make your name great, so that you will be a blessing. I will bless those who bless you, and the one who curses you I will curse; and in you all the families of the earth shall be blessed. Genesis 12: 2–3

married to Abraham, expelled them both, with their flocks, from Egypt.

Abraham returned to Canaan, where he settled at Mamre, close to Hebron. Once again, God promised Abraham that he would support him, and that the land in which he was living would one day belong to his descendants.

The birth of Ishmael
Abraham feared God could not keep this promise because Sarah was barren. Following local custom, Sarah told Abraham to sleep with her maid, Hagar. But when Hagar became pregnant, Sarah drove her out into the desert. There Hagar was rescued by an angel and she returned to Abraham's household to have her son, Ishmael. God then told Abraham that for the land to pass to his descendants, he must be circumcised and lead a pure life, and God would then give him and Sarah a son.

The procession (below) of men with sheep, goats, and bullocks shows the sort of stock that Abraham would have taken with him into Canaan. This frieze is from Ur, in southern Mesopotamia, where Abraham lived before moving with his family to Haran.

Abraham's Journey
At the time he heard God's call, Abraham was living near the city of Haran in northern Mesopotamia. The Bible does not say how long Abraham had lived there, although it does relate how he had been brought up near Ur, in Sumer, and had traveled north with his wife, Sarah, his father, Terah, and his nephew, Lot. Leaving Haran, Abraham's route probably took him across the Euphrates, then south past Damascus to Bethel. He then continued south to the Negeb, but this semidesert provided little food for his animals. Soon a famine forced Abraham to move on to Egypt.

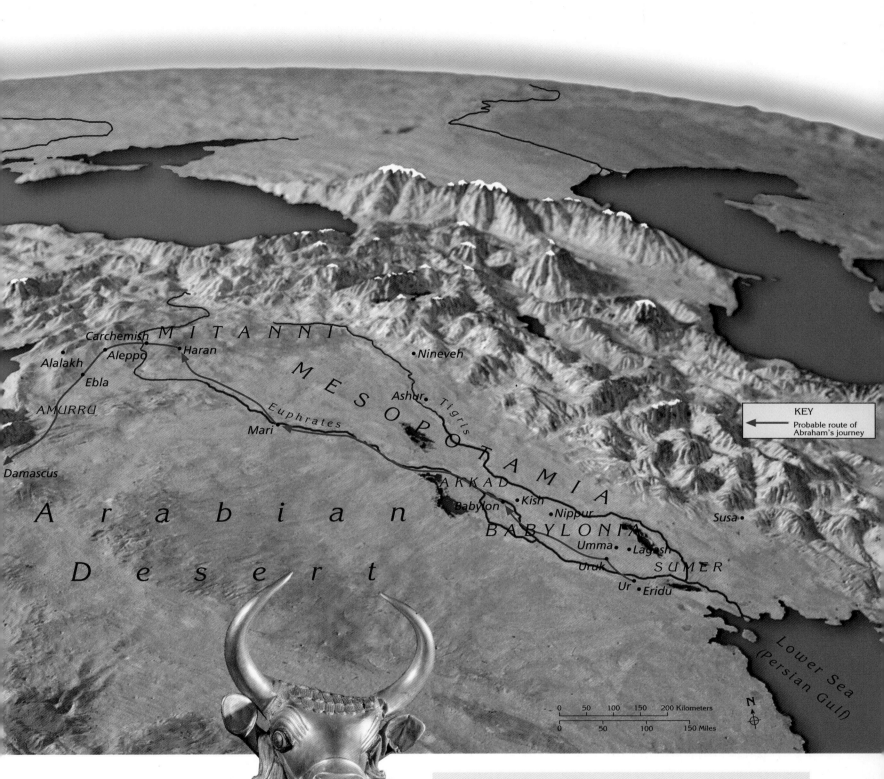

Carchemish
Alalakh
Aleppo • Haran
Ebla
AMURRU
MITANNI
Nineveh
MESOPOTAMIA
Ashur • Tigris
Euphrates
Mari
Damascus
A r a b i a n
AKKAD
Babylon • Kish
• Nippur
Susa •
B A B Y L O N I A
D e s e r t
Umma • Lagash
Uruk • SUMER
Ur • Eridu
Lower Sea (Persian Gulf)

KEY
Probable route of
Abraham's journey

0   50   100   150   200 Kilometers
0   50   100   150 Miles

N

Abraham and his family *seem to have been seminomadic, like many Bedouin of today. They settled in an area, but moved when necessary to find new pastures for their animals.*

The wealth of Ur *is evident in this finely sculpted gold head of a bull, which was made to decorate a lyre – a stringed instrument that was played throughout the Middle East.*

The Destruction of Sodom

One day three visitors dined with Abraham at his tent near Mamre in Canaan. As they were leaving, the visitors told Abraham that God was about to destroy the cities of Sodom and Gomorrah because of the wickedness of their inhabitants. Abraham pleaded with God to spare the cities, but God decreed that only Abraham's nephew, Lot, and his family, living at Sodom, were worthy of being saved. Warned of the coming disaster by two angels, Lot fled with his wife and two daughters, but his wife ignored the angels' warning not to look back as the cities were destroyed and was promptly turned into a pillar of salt. This part of the story may well have been influenced by the eerie natural salt formations found scattered around the Dead Sea (below).

Abraham's Covenant

The figure of Abraham, a pious man from near Ur in southern Mesopotamia, features prominently in Judaism, Christianity, and Islam. All three religions regard him as the father of the faithful. God made a covenant, or agreement, with Abraham, promising that he would have many descendants who would be given a homeland in return for faith and obedience. To be sure of Abraham's worthiness, God twice put him to the test and on both occasions Abraham proved himself.

The first test was of Abraham's faith. One day, when Abraham was living at Mamre, near Hebron, three strangers visited him. After Abraham had welcomed them and given them a meal, the strangers warned him about the impending destruction of the wicked cities of Sodom and Gomorrah near the Dead Sea. They also

astonished Abraham by saying that his wife, Sarah, who was old and had never borne children, would soon have a son. Incredible though it seemed, Abraham believed the strangers, and a year later his faith was rewarded when Sarai gave birth to a boy, whom they named Isaac.

The second trial concerned Abraham's obedience. When Isaac reached boyhood, God told Abraham to offer him up as a sacrifice. Abraham obeyed without question, taking Isaac to the place appointed – traditionally identified with Mount Moriah in Jerusalem. When Isaac asked where was the lamb for sacrifice, Abraham said that God would provide. He built an altar and laid his son upon it. As he raised his knife to kill Isaac, Abraham heard an angel telling him to stop. He looked round, and seeing a ram caught fast in a bush, sacrificed that instead.

After this confirmation of Abraham's faith and obedience, God affirmed his covenant with him, promising Abraham many descendants through whom all nations would be blessed.

Above: Abraham prepares to sacrifice Isaac in a mosaic from the Beth-alpha synagogue.
Background: Judean desert south of Hebron.
Map: Area around Hebron in which Abraham lived.

1. The Great Mosque at Hebron, site of Abraham's tomb.
2. Dead Sea salt formations.
3. Gold bull's head from Ur.
4. Sheep flocks in the desert.
5. Clay column, with the names of Abraham and his descendants.

Jerusalem

Mamre
Hebron

Salt
Sea
(Dead
Sea)

3

4

5

Egyptian tomb painting of traders from Asia

Before he died, Abraham saw his son Isaac married to Rebekah, a relative from near Haran. Rebekah bore Isaac twins: Esau, the boisterous first born, a hunter, and the favorite of his father; and the quiet, clever Jacob, favored by his mother. Jacob had a ruthless, ambitious streak in him. One day Esau came home from hunting, weak with hunger, to find Jacob cooking a stew. Jacob refused to feed him any until Esau agreed to give him his birthright in return – entitling Jacob to the inheritance of his brother and the future headship of the family.

Later, with Rebekah's connivance, Jacob deceived his father in an even more devious manner. Isaac, who was by now old and blind, asked Esau to prepare him a meal. But Jacob himself took Isaac the food. Isaac was suspicious and

> ■ Be fruitful and multiply; a nation and a company of nations shall come from you, and kings shall spring from you. The land that I gave to Abraham and Isaac I will give to you, and I will give the land to your offspring after you.
>
> Genesis 35:11–12

asked to touch him. But Jacob had dressed himself in goat skins to impersonate his brother's hairy skin. Isaac was convinced, and gave Jacob his blessing – thereby passing on the spirit and leadership of the family to the younger son.

The journey to Haran

Esau planned to kill Jacob once their father was dead, but Rebekah sent Jacob away to safety in Haran, where she hoped he would find a wife. On the way Jacob lay down in the open to sleep, with a stone for his pillow, and dreamed that he saw a ladder leading up to heaven. Angels were going up and down the ladder, and God stood at its top. God told Jacob that he would give all the surrounding land to his descendants and that he would watch over him during his journey and bring him back safely to Canaan. When Jacob awoke, he named the place of this sacred dream Bethel, and marked it by setting up an anointed stone pillar.

On reaching Haran, Jacob met his uncle Laban's younger daughter Rachel at a well and fell in love with her. In return for Rachel's hand in marriage, Laban made Jacob work for seven years as his shepherd. But at the wedding it was Jacob's turn to be tricked, and he woke up the next morning beside Laban's elder daughter, Leah. Jacob was furious, but Laban agreed that for another seven years' work Jacob could marry Rachel as well. During his years of toil, Jacob built up his own flocks, and after marrying Rachel he returned to Canaan with his wives, children, and animals.

***This Canaanite pottery** dates from 1500–1200 BCE, and is a fine example of decorated household ware of the time.*

Jacob's Journey
The exact route of Jacob's journey to and from Haran is not stated in the Bible, although he is likely to have followed one of the major trade routes that connected Canaan with Mesopotamia.

Elath

Mesopotamian Cities
The alabaster statue (right), dating from about 1800 BCE, was found at Mari, on the upper Euphrates. Mari was the most powerful city in the region at the time when Jacob fled to Haran to escape the wrath of his brother Esau. The statue depicts the chief official of the temple of the goddess Astarte. Both Mari and Haran were commercial and religious centers that lay on major trade routes linking Mesopotamia and the west.

Great Sea
(Mediterranean)

Carchemish

Aleppo

Haran

Euphrates

PADDAN-
ARAM

Batih

Hamath

Qatna

Habor

Tigris

MESOPOTAMIA

Hazor

Damascus

Megiddo

Dothan

Shechem

Jordan

GILEAD

Ashtaroth-karnaim

Mari

Euphrates

Shiloh

Succoth

Ramoth-gilead

Jerusalem

Jabbok

Penuel

Bethel

Mahanaim

Hebron

CANAAN

Ephrath (Bethlehem)

*Salt Sea
(Dead Sea)*

Beersheba

EDOM

0   50   100   150 Kilometers

0   25   50   75   100 Miles

Clay figurines *of the goddess
Astarte. The Canaanites
revered a pantheon of gods and
goddesses.*

Return to Canaan

Jacob was very much afraid of meeting his brother Esau
again, and he spent the night before their reunion alone. In
his sleep, a mysterious stranger came and wrestled with him
all night. By daybreak, Jacob had still not succumbed and the
stranger, an angel of God, decreed that Jacob would now be
called Israel – 'The one who strives with God' – because he
had struggled with God and with humans and had triumphed.

Jacob and Esau were reconciled. Jacob moved to Bethel
and built an altar at the place where God had first spoken to
him. Eventually he and his family moved to Egypt to be with
Joseph, his first son by his beloved wife, Rachel. Jacob lived
his last days there in quiet piety, his final act being to bless his
12 sons, who became the ancestors of the 12 tribes of Israel.

Joseph dreaming – from a Hebrew manuscript

Joseph, the child of Jacob by his beloved wife Rachel, was his father's favorite. When Jacob gave Joseph an ornamented robe with sleeves, or 'coat of many colours,' his 11 brothers became jealous because of the preference shown by their father. Joseph made matters worse by telling them about two of his dreams. In the first, Joseph and his brothers were binding sheaves of grain, and the brothers' sheaves all bowed down to Joseph's sheaf. In the second dream, 11 stars, the sun and the moon – which Joseph interpreted as representing his brothers, his father, and his mother – bowed down to him.

The brothers' jealousy now turned to hatred and thoughts of murder. One day, just as they were about to carry out their heinous deed, they saw a caravan of traders taking spices down to Egypt. One brother, Judah, suggested that instead of killing Joseph, they should sell him as a slave. The others agreed, so they sold him to the traders for 20 shekels. After dipping Joseph's robe in goat's blood, they told their grieving father that Joseph must have been killed by a wild animal.

> ■ There will come seven years of great plenty throughout all the land of Egypt. After them there will arise seven years of famine, and all the plenty will be forgotten; the famine will consume the land.
>
> Genesis 41:29–30

Once in Egypt, Joseph was bought by Potiphar, the captain of the Pharaoh's guard. Joseph soon became head of Potiphar's entire household, and Potiphar's wife, who was attracted by the handsome young man, tried to seduce him. But Joseph rejected her advances, and in revenge she falsely accused him of trying to rape her.

When Potiphar heard this he locked Joseph up with the Pharaoh's other prisoners. While in prison, Joseph interpreted the dreams of two of Pharaoh's former servants, a baker and a cupbearer, saying that the first would be executed, while the second would soon be restored to favor at court. Everything turned out as Joseph had predicted, and Joseph asked the cupbearer to speak to the Pharaoh on his behalf. But once free, the cupbearer forgot Joseph's plea.

The Pharaoh's dreams

Two years later the Pharaoh himself had two strange dreams, which none of his magicians could understand. Only then did the cupbearer remember Joseph, and he was hastily brought into the Pharaoh's presence.

In the first of the Pharaoh's dreams, seven sleek, fat cows were grazing among the reeds of the Nile, when seven ugly, scrawny cows came and ate them up, but still remained as thin as before. In the second dream the Pharaoh saw seven good ears of grain, which were swallowed up by seven thin, blighted ears of grain. Immediately, Joseph said that both dreams were a warning that seven years of plenty would be followed by seven years of famine. Joseph suggested that enough food should be stored during the good years to avoid famine during the bad.

The Pharaoh was so impressed that he made Joseph his chief minister. During the good years, Joseph built up great stocks of food. In the subsequent time of famine, the storehouses were opened and the people were fed.

However, the famine spread beyond Egypt to Canaan, and soon Joseph's brothers arrived to buy grain. Recognizing them, Joseph questioned them about his family and eventually told them who he was. He told them not be afraid, as he believed God had sent him ahead to Egypt to save his kinsmen from starvation. With the Pharaoh's permission, Joseph's whole family came to Egypt, where they settled in an area called Goshen – probably in the eastern Nile delta.

Hyksos rule in Egypt
It is possible that the story of Joseph relates to the period after 1700 BCE, when Egypt was ruled by the Hyksos people from Canaan. These people might have appointed a non-Egyptian as chief minister. This map shows the extent of Hyksos rule and the possible route of the traders who brought Joseph to Egypt.

The harvesting of crops, *as shown in an Egyptian tomb painting. The most common grain crops of the time were barley and emmer wheat, used for brewing and bread-making.*

Bread made from *emmer wheat was the staple food for most people in ancient Egypt. This clay figurine shows a man (maybe a miller) grinding wheat to make flour.*

N

G r e a t
S e a
(Mediterranean)

Buto
WEST Sais
DELTA EAST
DELTA
Bubastis
Athribis Tanis Sile
Ro-waty GOSHEN
Memphis Avaris
On (Heliopolis)
Herakleopolis
Nile

Beth-shean
Dothan
Sea of Galilee
Shechem
Joppa
Ashkelon
Beersheba
Lachish GILEAD
Jericho
Hebron
RETENU
(CANAAN) Salt Sea
(Dead Sea)

SINAI

R e d
S e a

KEY
Hyksos border
Canaan under Hyksos influence
Route of Hyksos
Joseph's journey from Hebron to Dothan
Route of Midian traders

The Pharaoh's vizier, or chief minister, sits before a table piled high with food (right). Joseph was appointed to the position of vizier after impressing the Pharaoh with his interpretation of dreams. The clay model (top right) shows an Egyptian grain silo with a woman grinding wheat while a scribe keeps records of the amount of grain in storage. Joseph was in overall charge of food supplies during the seven years of plenty and seven years of famine in Egypt.

In the centuries after the death of Joseph, the Israelites were more and more repressed by the rulers of Egypt. By the time of Pharaohs Sethos I and Rameses II, in the 13th century BCE, they had become virtual slave laborers.

The Bible tells how the Pharaoh was alarmed by the rising numbers of the Israelites and decreed that every Israelite boy be killed at birth. In an attempt to save her baby, one woman, Jochebed, hid her infant son in a papyrus basket among the reeds along the banks of the Nile, tending to him secretly. Some time afterward, the Pharaoh's daughter came to bathe and discovered the basket. She took pity on the child, thinking he had been abandoned, and brought him to live in the royal court as her own son. She named the boy Moses.

The Bible says nothing about Moses' upbringing at court, although he is traditionally said to have spent some 40 years there. Eventually, Moses found out that he was an Israelite, not an Egyptian, and was shocked by the hard labor required of his kinsmen. When he saw an Egyptian beating an Israelite, Moses killed the man and hid his body in the desert, but his crime was soon discovered and he fled to Sinai. Here he took refuge with Jethro, a priest, and became a shepherd. It was

A mosaic of Moses wearing Roman garb

■ I am the Lord, and I will free you from the burdens of the Egyptians ... with mighty acts of judgment.

Exodus 6:6

while tending his sheep that Moses first encountered the power and presence of God. One day Moses saw a bush which was apparently consumed by flames but miraculously did not burn. As Moses drew near to the bush, the voice of God spoke from it, instructing him to lead the Israelites out of Egypt and servitude. Moses protested that he was not worthy of the task, but God insisted, assuring Moses of his help.

Ten plagues

Moses returned to Egypt and, with his older brother Aaron, won the support of the Israelites. They then met with the Pharaoh – probably Rameses II – to ask that their people be allowed to leave Egypt to offer sacrifices in the desert. The Pharaoh refused. In response, God sent a succession of ten plagues upon the Egyptians. He turned the Nile into blood and sent hordes of frogs, gnats, and flies. The Pharaoh repeatedly made promises, only to break them. In response, God sent further pestilences: disease upon the Pharaoh's livestock, boils upon his people and animals, hail and locusts to destroy his crops, and total darkness over Egypt for three days. When the Pharaoh broke his word again, God imposed a tenth plague, which finally broke the Pharaoh's resolve.

This Egyptian mural *(above) shows bird-hunting in papyrus beds along the banks of the River Nile. The Bible says that Moses' basket was woven from this versatile plant. The 'reeds' among which the Bible says the basket was hidden were also probably papyrus.*

Tombo
Kerma
Kawa
Napata

The Israelites, *and other foreigners living in Egypt, provided the manpower (below) that enabled the Pharaohs of the time to build their great monuments, cities, temples, and palaces.*

Carchemish
Alalakh
Ugarit
Aleppo
Hamath
Byblos
Qadesh
Sidon
Tyre
Megiddo
Damascus
Gezer
Shechem
Gaza
Jerusalem
Hebron
Salt Sea (Dead Sea)
C A N A A N

Buto
Piramesses
Tanis
Bubastis
Memphis
Pithom
LOWER EGYPT
Herakleopolis
El-Ashmunein
SINAI
Western Desert
Nile
Eastern Desert
El-Amarna
UPPER
Asyut
Abydos Akhmim
Armant Thebes
EGYPT
Hierakonopolis
El-Kab
Edfu
Elephantine

Red Sea

Buhen
Semna
Nile
NUBIA
KUSH

KEY
Border under Thutmose III
Border under Rameses II

0
50
100
100
150
200
300 Kilometers
200 Miles

Egyptian New Kingdom
During the time of Moses, the Egyptian New Kingdom dominated a vast swathe of land. At its greatest extent, New Kingdom territory stretched from Nubia in the south to the Carchemish on the Euphrates in the north, and included the land of Canaan.

The legendary Nile, the banks of which provided a temporary hiding place for the infant Moses until he was discovered by the Pharaoh's daughter and taken into her care.

The temple at Karnak in Upper Egypt gives some idea of the impressive monumental building work the Israelites were forced to undertake for their Egyptian masters.

The waters part to allow the Israelites to cross

When the Pharoah refused Moses' request to allow the Israelites to leave Egypt, God sent a series of nine plagues to force his hand – but he would not relent. Finally, God decreed that he would inflict a tenth plague so severe that the Pharaoh would have to let the Israelites go. At midnight, every firstborn male in the land, be he prince, servant, or even beast, would die. To escape the slaughter, the Israelites were to mark the frames of their doorposts with lambs' blood as a signal to the Angel of Death to pass by. The Israelites ate a solemn meal of meat roasted with bitter herbs and waited. When midnight came, God duly struck down every Egyptian firstborn male including the Pharaoh's own son. The Pharaoh summoned Moses and his brother Aaron and told them to leave with all their animals and belongings. He gave them gifts of gold and silver and even asked for their blessing. Free at last, the Israelites headed southeast toward Succoth. Their exact route from then on, across the Sinai Peninsula, is unknown except that they avoided traveling through areas dominated by likely hostile peoples such as the Philistines.

Into the desert

It is unclear how many people Moses actually led out of Egypt but an estimate of 6000 men, together with their wives

■ Has any god ever attempted to go and take a nation for himself from the midst of another nation, by trials, by signs and wonders... and by terrifying displays of power, as the Lord your God did for you in Egypt ... ?

Deuteronomy 4:34

and children, is probably a reasonable one. They traveled continuously, led by a pillar of cloud by day and a pillar of fire by night, until they came to a sea, often described as the 'Red Sea,' where they set up camp. This was probably a shallow lake – in Hebrew a 'Sea of Reeds' – rather than the Red Sea itself which is a long way south of their most likely routes across the desert. Here the Egyptian army caught up with them. The Pharaoh had changed his mind and decided he did not, after all, wish to lose his valuable Israelite workforce, and had sent his troops in hot pursuit.

Terrified, the Israelites turned on Moses, accusing him of leading them into destruction. Moses called on God who instructed him to stretch out his hand over the sea. When Moses did so, God drove the waters back with a strong wind and the Israelites crossed to the other side. The Egyptians followed closely behind, but their chariot wheels became embedded in the mud. Then Moses again held out his hand and the waters returned, sweeping the Egyptians to oblivion.

The Pharaoh's troops were able to catch up with the fleeing Israelites by using swift, horse-drawn war chariots, such as the one pictured above. Although the chariots were relatively light, they and the horses still sank into the mud when they tried to pursue the Israelites across the 'Sea of Reeds.' Unable to escape when God closed the waters over them, men and horses alike were swept to a watery grave.

The Israelites escaped from the Egyptians at a 'Sea of Reeds' perhaps similar to this area of the Nile Delta (above left). Reeds grow thickly along the banks of the Nile and were a haven for waterfowl, as shown in this wall painting (above right). It is impossible to say exactly where the 'Sea of Reeds' was, although a mistranslation of the original Hebrew means it has traditionally become associated with the Red Sea.

Map labels

Great Sea (Mediterranean)

Lake Menzaleh
Baal-zephon?
Lake Sirbonis
Pirameses
Etham
Migdol
The Way to the Land of the Philistines
Pithom
Succoth
GOSHEN
EGYPT
On (Heliopolis)
Lake Timsah
Great Bitter Lake
Baal-zephon?
Little Bitter Lake
Memphis
Wilderness of Shur
The Way to Shur
Ashdod
Ashkelon
Gaza
Plain of Philistia
CANAAN
Jericho
Jordan
Hormah
Hebron
Salt Sea (Dead Sea)
Mt Nebo
Dibon
Arad
Negeb
MOAB
Azmon
Bene-Jaakan (Beeroth)
Wilderness of Zin
Kadesh-barnea
Oboth
Punon
EDOM
THE ARABAH
SINAI
Wilderness of Paran
Wilderness of Sin?
Mt Sinai (Horeb)?
Ezion-geber
MIDIAN
Mt Sinai (Horeb)?
Gulf of Suez
Gulf of Akaba
Red Sea

KEY
Traditional Exodus route
Possible northern Exodus route
Alternative Exodus route

The Exodus
Experts disagree on the exact route taken by the Israelites out of Egypt, as the account in Exodus is unclear. They either walked across the Wilderness of Shur or headed south around the Sinai Peninsula. Neither route was direct or easy.

The Passover
In ancient times, oil lamps such as this were lit during the feast of the Passover, which celebrates God's deliverance of the Israelites from Egypt. The name of the festival refers to the Angel of

Death 'passing over' the homes of the Israelites on the night of the tenth plague. That evening, every Israelite family had a hearty meal of goat or lamb roasted with bitter herbs and eaten with unleavened bread, so that they would not be hungry at the outset of their journey.

Life in the Desert

The Israelites would have spent long enough in Egypt to forget their previous nomadic lifestyle and how to cope with the rigors of desert life. Perhaps the only one among them to have recent experience of this testing environment was Moses, after his years as a desert shepherd.

The Bible tells how the Israelites left Egypt with their sheep, goats, and cattle, so they needed to be constantly on the move in search of grazing. They may have been like the nomadic Bedouin of today living in tents and swathed in layers of clothes against the elements.

The Israelites' greatest problem was water. In their wanderings in the Desert of Shur, they traveled for several days finding only one source of water, at Marah, which was undrinkable. On this occasion, the Bible tells

how God directed Moses to throw a piece of wood into the water and this miraculously purified it. At Rephidim near Mount Sinai, the people were so desperate for water that they were about to stone Moses in anger because he had brought them to this desolate place. But the Lord told Moses to strike a rock with his staff and water gushed out. Later when the Israelites were camped in Moab, God caused a well to open up in the dry desert.

Food was also difficult to find. The Israelites missed the plentiful provisions of Egypt and again blamed Moses for taking them away, forgetting that they had been released from servitude. In answer God sent quails and manna – a strange food which appeared as fresh flakes every morning but melted away by noon. While finding water and flocks of migratory birds in the desert can readily be explained, scholars have yet to agree on what manna might actually have been.

Above: Moses and the miraculous well in Moab, from a wall painting in the Dura-Europos synagogue.
Background: Judean desert.
Map: Rephidim, where Moses struck water from a rock.

1. A dry desolate region of mountainous central Sinai.
2. Precious water collected in a serene pool below Mount Sinai.
3. Sunrise at Mount Sinai.
4. Central Sinai.

Bronze Egyptian statuette of a calf

In the third month after leaving Egypt, the Israelites reached Mount Sinai. Here, Moses gathered the people together and they watched fearfully as God descended onto the summit of Mount Sinai in a thick cloud, accompanied by thunder and lightning. God then summoned Moses to the top of the mountain, where he gave him the Ten Commandments on tablets of stone. He also laid down numerous other laws that the Israelites were required to obey. When Moses passed on these laws and everything else that God had instructed, the people all shouted out their agreement, thereby accepting the covenant of the Lord.

Moses climbed Mount Sinai again to receive instructions on how the sacred tablets were to be kept. God told him to construct a chest made of acacia wood and gold – the Ark of the Covenant. This was to hold the tablets and would itself be housed in a tabernacle, a portable holy sanctuary, which the Israelites would carry with them.

Moses was away for 40 days, and in his absence many people became unsettled. They persuaded Moses' brother, Aaron, to make them an idol that they could worship. Aaron obliged by melting down their jewelry and fashioning a golden calf from it. When Moses came down from the mountain and saw the people dancing round the calf, he

■ You have seen what I did to the Egyptians ... Now therefore, if you obey my voice and keep my covenant, you shall be my treasured possession out of all the peoples.
Exodus 19:4–5

threw down the tablets in anger, smashing them to pieces. Summoning those who were still true to God, Moses ordered that all worshipers of the calf should be killed.

Within sight of Canaan

God wrote the Commandments again on two more tablets, and before the Israelites left for Canaan he instructed Moses on how to keep the laws he had laid down. The Israelites then resumed their journey and as they approached Canaan, Moses sent out spies to explore. They discovered a land flowing with milk and honey but found the inhabitants to be hostile. On hearing this the people rebelled, saying that they would never conquer Canaan and demanding to return to Egypt. Angry at their lack of faith, God declared that the generation that had left Egypt would never enter the Promised Land. He condemned them to wander for 40 years in the wilderness until the next generation was ready to take possession of Canaan.

Moses continued as chief of the Israelites but God did not permit him to lead his people into Canaan – that task would fall to another. Instead he allowed Moses only a glimpse of the Promised Land, just before his death, from atop Mount Nebo.

Exodus gives precise details about the construction of the Ark of the Covenant and the tabernacle where it was kept. The Ark was placed behind a curtain (above left) at the back of the tabernacle. In front of the curtain stood a menorah, or candlestick, typically with seven branches (above right).

From Mount Nebo (above), Moses was allowed by God to glimpse the Promised Land before he died at the age of 120. To his west was the Dead Sea, with the Judean hills beyond; to the north lay the River Jordan, which the Israelites would have to cross when they finally entered Canaan.

The Breastplate of Judgment

The 12 tribes of Israel that followed Moses out of Egypt were descended from Jacob's 12 sons. Each tribe was represented by a precious stone on the 'Breastplate of Judgment' – part of the High Priest's ceremonial dress – arranged in four rows of three. Thus, when he entered the Holy of Holies in the tabernacle – he being the only person permitted to do so – the High Priest symbolically took the 12 tribes with him.

The Tabernacle
The Ark of the Covenant was housed in the tabernacle. This was a portable sanctuary, like a tent, which stood within a large, open courtyard surrounded by curtains. The tabernacle was eventually replaced by a permanent temple once the Israelites had finally settled in Canaan.

The tabernacle

Wall of curtains, held up by bronze posts and silver rods

Holy of Holies, or Most Holy Place, containing the Ark of the Covenant

Altar for sacrificial burnt offerings

Bronze basin for ritual washing

The Ten Commandments
share many features with the Hammurabi Code, drawn up by Hammurabi, king of Babylon from c.1792–1750 BCE. The code was written on a 2m (7 ft) high stone monument, or stele (above) found at Susa, an early Babylonian city.

Moses was destined never to lead his people into the Promised Land. This task was to fall to his closest associate, the faithful Joshua, who had never doubted that, with God's help, the Israelites would enter Canaan. Before his death, Moses passed on the leadership to Joshua in front of the assembled tribes of Israel. Once Moses had died, God told Joshua that the time had now come to lead his people across the River Jordan and into Canaan. He urged Joshua to be strong and courageous and promised to be with him throughout the daunting time ahead.

The land of Canaan that God had promised to the Israelites was already settled by a people who worshiped their own gods, and the Lord decreed that the Israelites would have to invade and conquer these people in order to claim the

**Bronze
Canaanite
sword**

land as their own. The first stage of this invasion was the crossing of the River Jordan, and Joshua immediately ordered his officers to prepare the people for this. Meanwhile, he sent spies on ahead to the nearby Canaanite citadel of Jericho. There the spies took refuge in the house of a woman called Rahab, who may also have been a prostitute. Rahab told the spies that the people of Jericho 'melt in fear' at the thought of the approach of the Israelites. She then helped them to escape from the city and return to Joshua. In exchange, they promised that she and her family would be spared when the Israelites finally attacked Jericho.

Into Canaan

Delighted at the news that his spies had brought him, Joshua gave orders to cross the river, which was then in full spate. He instructed the priests to go in front, bearing the Ark of the

■ Be strong ... for you shall put these people in possession of the land that I swore to their ancestors to give them.

Joshua 1:6

Covenant. As soon as the priests had stepped into the swollen river, the turbulent waters abated. While the priests stayed firmly in the middle of the riverbed, it remained dry and the people were able to cross. Representatives of the 12 tribes of Israel each took a stone from the dry riverbed as they crossed and piled them up into a cairn on the bank as a reminder to future generations of God's power. After the priests had finally carried the Ark out of the river, the waters returned, flowing as strongly as ever.

Once they were all safely across the River Jordan, the Israelites pitched camp and celebrated the Passover. God told Joshua that the people were at last fit to be given the Promised Land. All was now ready for them to attack their first target, the city of Jericho.

The River Jordan (above) was not a strict political boundary; nevertheless, the act of crossing it was a critical moment, representing the entry of the Israelites into the Promised Land. Stopping the flow of the river in spring, when it was in full flood, made the event even more noteworthy.

The Ark of the Covenant, here represented in a stone sculpture, had a great religious and symbolic significance, as it housed the tablets of the Ten Commandments and other holy relics. The Ark was made of acacia wood and gold, with a lid of solid gold. It was believed that God was invisibly enthroned within the Ark.

Great Sea

Lower Beth-horon
Upper Beth-horon
Ashdod Ekron
Makkedah?
Gath Azekah
Ashkelon
Libnah
Gaza Eglon Lachish
Hebron

C

Salt

N e g e b

E D O M

0   10   20 Kilometers
0   10   20 Miles

Sidon

Baal-gad?

Mt Hermon

Tyre

Kedesh

Merom

Hazor

Waters of Merom

Achshaph

Sea of Galilee

Shimron

Megiddo

Valley of Jezreel

Mt Ebal

Mt Gerizim

Shechem

Jabbok

Adam

Bethel

Ai

Jericho

Gilgal

Gibeon

Shittim

Jerusalem

Jarmuth

Valley of Achor

(Dead Sea)

Dibon

(Mediterranean)

Jordan

AMMON

MOAB

KEY

* 5 Philistine cities not captured
+ Towns captured by Joshua
✗ Battle site

Over the Jordan

After their journey north through Moab, the Israelites turned west and crossed the River Jordan. The exact site of their crossing is unknown, but was probably about 25km (16 miles) north of Jericho at Adam, close to where the River Jabbok joins the Jordan. The Bible records the river as drying up. This could have occurred as the result of a landslide. In 1927 an earthquake caused a landslide which blocked the waters of the Jordan for more than 21 hours.

The Canaanites

The Canaanites' civilization flourished in cities such as Jerusalem and Jericho from about 2000 to 1550 BCE. They worshiped many gods and goddesses, most notably Baal, whose name means 'Lord' or 'Master.' Baal was believed to bring rain and fertility to the land. He is often shown holding a club, presumably lost from this gold-and-bronze figure (right), dating from between 1400 and 1200 BCE. The clay fertility goddess figurines and the molds from which they were cast (below) are often found in excavations of the private houses of the period, and were probably worshiped by women.

A Mesopotamian trumpeter

The Israelites had reached the Promised Land of Canaan and were now preparing to conquer its inhabitants. Their first challenge was the capture of the Canaanite citadel of Jericho. God instructed them to march in silence for six days around Jericho's stout walls, carrying the Ark of the Covenant. Seven priests blowing trumpets of rams' horns were to lead the procession. This they did until the seventh day, when they circled the city seven times. The priests gave a final blast on the trumpets and the Israelites broke their silence, giving a loud shout, and the walls of Jericho collapsed, allowing the invaders to pour into the city.

God ordered that every living thing there was to be put to the sword. Only the family of Rahab – the woman who had earlier hidden Israelite spies sent to reconnoiter the city – was saved from the massacre. All the city's silver, gold, bronze, and iron was collected in the name of the Lord, and the Israelites were warned by God to take nothing for themselves. Jericho was then burned to the ground and Joshua cursed the site so that the city was never rebuilt there.

■ As soon as the people heard the sound of the trumpets, they raised a great shout, and the wall fell down flat; so the people charged straight ahead into the city and captured it.
Joshua 6:20

News of Joshua's magnificent victory at Jericho spread rapidly, and the Canaanites were fearful of what he and the Israelites would do next. By following the drastic method of extermination of the enemy, coupled with the destruction or confiscation of all property, Joshua sent out a powerful message to other cities in Canaan that they should surrender to the Israelites if they wished to survive.

The campaign continues
After his success at Jericho, Joshua sent spies to the nearby city of Ai which he had selected as his next target. On their return the spies reported confidently that very few men would be needed to take the city. Encouraged, Joshua sent a small army of around 3000, but to his horror, the Israelites were routed; many were killed and those that returned were full of fear. Joshua prostrated himself before God and begged to know why he had failed. God replied that one man had disobeyed his orders at the sack of Jericho, having taken precious articles for himself instead of giving them all up to the Lord. Joshua called forward the 12 tribes of Israel and by a process of elimination finally discovered the culprit – a man named Achan from the tribe of Judah. When Joshua

questioned him he discovered that Achan had indeed stolen gold and silver coins, together with valuable robes, and had hidden them beneath his tent.

Joshua ordered that both Achan and his family be stoned to death in retribution for such treachery. In this way, Joshua showed that neither he nor God was prepared to tolerate any disobedience from the Israelites that might jeopardize their conquering of the Promised Land.

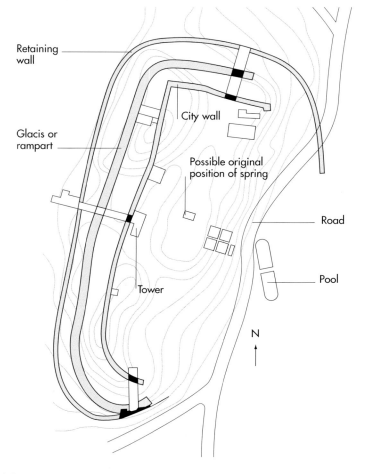

The ancient city of Jericho was originally sited around a spring which provided a natural water source. Jericho dates back to c.8000 BCE when it was home to around 1500 people. Excavations of the city mound have revealed layer upon layer of buildings. As each building fell into disrepair, it was knocked down and a new one built on top, thus gradually raising the level of the city.

With its bulging eyes, large ears, prominent nose, and narrow chin, this striking pottery vessel is one of the most remarkable artefacts found at Jericho. Known as Tell el-Yahudiyeh ware, this particular example was probably a cup used for special ceremonial occasions.

The Ancestors

Archeological evidence from Jericho suggests that its people may have worshiped their ancestors. Families buried the bodies of dead relatives under the floors of their houses. The heads were treated differently. They were removed and the flesh was allowed to rot away. Then the dead person's features were restored in clay molded over the skull and sometimes painted with a flesh-coloured tint. The eye sockets were filled with shells. It is unclear why this was done. Perhaps the people of Jericho hoped to preserve the wisdom of their ancestors; or perhaps they simply wanted to keep the generations of the family together, the living dwelling with the dead.

The site of the city of Jericho as it appears today in an aerial view from the north. Layers of successive building created this large mound; its hummocky surface reflects the outlines of ancient buildings as well as recent excavations.

This round tower, attached to the inside of Jericho's original city walls, dates from c.7000 BCE. It is 10m (33 ft) in diameter and 8m (26 ft) tall. The most likely function of this structure was as a watchtower, although this is not confirmed.

Ditch

City wall

Glacis, or rampart, covered with plaster

The City of Jericho

This reconstruction of Jericho shows how the plaster glacis, or rampart, might have looked. The city stood on an artificial mound encircled by a wall made of mudbrick. Around the base was a ditch and a stone supporting wall. A surface layer of plaster stabilized the sides of the earth mound.

A Canaanite cult mask found in Galilee

The Israelites failed in their first assault on the Canaanite city of Ai, but encouraged by God Joshua led a large army back there and routed the defenders by luring them into a clever ambush. First, he drew the men of Ai away from their city by feigning a retreat. A second Israelite contingent then entered the undefended city, set it on fire, before rushing forward to help their main army. Once the 'retreating' Israelite troops saw the smoke from Ai, they turned on the pursuing enemy, destroying them totally.

At this time, Canaan was not a unified country. It was more a loose confederation of small, independent kingdoms, each ruled from a major fortified city. On hearing that Jericho, and now Ai, had fallen, many of these local kings banded together to resist the Israelite advance. In contrast, the people of Gibeon to the northwest of Jerusalem, avoided open conflict with Joshua by deceiving him into thinking that they were not hostile neighbors, but strangers from a distant country. They negotiated a treaty with Joshua, agreeing to become his servants in return for their lives. Joshua soon discovered that the Gibeonites had tricked him, but he honored his promise, sparing their lives and making them servants of the Israelites.

Alarmed by the pact that the Gibeonites had made with the invaders, the king of Jerusalem called upon the kings of

> ■ So Joshua took all that land ... He took all their kings, struck them down, and put them to death ...
>
> Joshua 11:16–17

Hebron, Jarmuth, Lachish, and Eglon to attack Gibeon. Joshua responded to the Gibeonites' plea for help and, during the ensuing battle, God came to his aid by sending a storm of lethal hailstones and causing the sun to stand still. The Canaanites were routed and their five kings killed.

Joshua's victories continue
Capitalizing on his success, Joshua rapidly took several southern strongholds, massacring their inhabitants but leaving their cities standing. He then turned his attention to the north. Here the king of Hazor, the main city in Upper Galilee, raised an enormous army at the Waters of Merom. This time the resourceful Israelites hamstrung the Canaanites' horses, burned their chariots, and put the enemy to flight. Hazor was captured and set ablaze, and the surrounding cities taken.

Although he had not conquered the whole of Canaan, Joshua had gained sufficient territory to divide between the 12 tribes of Israel. The Canaanites continued to offer sporadic resistance, but essentially the Promised Land was now, at last, under the dominion of Israel.

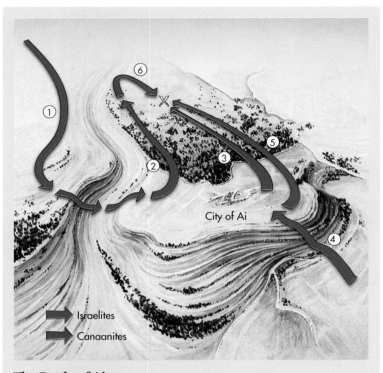

City of Ai

Israelites

Canaanites

The Battle of Ai
(1) Joshua's main army arrives from Jericho and approaches the city of Ai. It then feigns a retreat (2), which draws the soldiers of Ai out after it (3). (4) A second body of Israelites surges into the undefended city, massacring the inhabitants and setting the town on fire.

(5) These troops then rush to join the main army, which has seen the smoke of the burning town and turned on the Canaanites.In the ensuing battle (6), the army of Ai is totally annihilated by the Israelites.

The ruins of the city of Hazor in Galilee (below). According to the Bible, Hazor was one of the most important cities that Joshua razed in his campaign to conquer Canaan. He met the combined forces of Hazor and other neighboring kingdoms by the Waters of Merom and defeated them with ease.

Great Sea (Mediterranean)

Tyre

Dan

DAN

Acco

A S H E R

Waters of Meron

Hazor

Dor

ZEBULUN

N A P H T A L I

Sea of Galilee

Megiddo

ISSACHAR

Ashtaroth

Beth-shean

M A N A S S E H

Shechem

Joppa

E F R A I M

Shiloh

G
A
D

Upper Beth-horon

Lower Beth-horon

Bethel

Ashdod

Ekron

Gezer

Jordan

Ashkelon

Beth-shemesh

DAN

Gibeon

Ai

PHILISTIA

Gath

BENJAMIN

Gilgal

Jericho

Rabbah

Libnah

Jarmuth

Jerusalem

A M M O N

Eglon

Lachish

J U D A H

Ziklag

Hebron

R E U B E N

Beersheba

Salt Sea (Dead Sea)

ON

M O A B

0

0   60

25

50   120 Kilometers

E D O M   75 Miles

The settling of Canaan

This map shows how the land of Canaan was divided up between the 12 tribes of Israel following Joshua's successful invasion. Although Joshua did not conquer the whole of Canaan, it was not long before he had gained sufficient territory to allot areas to the 12 tribes. Most gained land to the west of the River Jordan.

Bronze-age weapons
comprising (left to right) a dagger blade and two spear heads, also a stone sling shot. Basic weapon design changed little over the centuries, and

although these examples are from an earlier period, both the Israelites and the Canaanites would have been armed with weapons of this type during the struggle for the Promised Land.

The Judges of Israel

Once the Israelites had entered Canaan under the leadership of Joshua, they came into frequent conflict with the local peoples. The Bible stresses how their success in overcoming this opposition – and their general prosperity – depended above all on their faith in and obedience to God. At various times of crisis the tribes of Israel united under the leadership of devout individuals known as 'Judges,' chosen by God to deliver them from their enemies.

Initially the Israelites occupied most of the hill country between the coastal plain and the Jordan Valley, where they enjoyed peace for 80 years after the Judge Ehud defeated the Moabites. This was followed by a period of 20 years when the Canaanite king of Hazor gained the upper hand. At the instigation of the

prophetess Deborah – the only known woman Judge – a man called Barak mustered 10,000 men at Mount Tabor overlooking the valley of Jezreel. At the ensuing battle by the waters of Megiddo, the Canaanites' heavy war chariots became bogged down in the mud and they were defeated. Their commander fled and hid in the tent of a woman called Jael, who killed him as he slept.

Some 40 years later the Israelites were plagued by camel-riding Midianite nomads who swooped down to plunder the Israelite lands at harvest time. Despite the Israelites' lapse into idolatry during this period, God gave them a leader, Gideon, to organize their resistance. Of the 32,000 men who rallied to his call, Gideon selected just 300. Arming them only with trumpets and torches, he led them to the Midianite camp. Then, at a prearranged signal, they blew their trumpets, brandished their torches and the Midianites panicked and fled.

In gratitude, the Israelites asked Gideon, a humble man, to become their ruler, but he declined, saying that God would rule them. Gideon's triumph brought his people 40 years of peace before conflict arose again with a new and formidable enemy, the Philistines.

Above: Deborah calls on Barak to oppose the Canaanites.
Background: Aerial view of traditional upland farmlands.
Map: Area of conflict between the Israelites and the Canaanites.

1. Megiddo fortress overlooking the Valley of Jezreel.
2. Canaanite image of a goddess.
3. Church of the Transfiguration on Mount Tabor.
4. Mount Tabor, Valley of Jezreel.

①

②

③

④

Bird-shaped offering bowl found in the third temple at Tell Qasile

In about 1200 BCE, the lands of the eastern Mediterranean were attacked by waves of 'Sea Peoples' from what is now Greece and western Turkey. One of these groups, the Philistines, started to settle along the coastal plain of Canaan in the area later known as Philistia – or as the Greeks called it, Palestine. Egyptian records claim that Pharaoh Rameses III (c.1183–1152 BCE) inflicted two severe defeats on the Philistines and other Sea Peoples in a struggle to maintain Egyptian domination of the region. Despite these reversals of fortune, the Philistines soon became firmly entrenched.

Contrary to popular perception, the Philistines had a highly developed culture. They were skilled metallurgists, and their pottery shows the influence of the advanced Mycenean civilization of Greece; many handsome beer mugs and wine cups have been excavated at Philistine sites. Their power was concentrated in a federation of five cities, each with its own lord: Gaza, Ashkelon, and Ashdod were on the coast, Gath and Ekron were inland. The Philistines' military skills, iron weapons and effective armor enabled them to subjugate the local Canaanite peoples, and then extend their control into adjoining Israelite lands. This domination provides the background to the Bible story of Samson.

Philistine religion

Details of Philistine religion are not clearly known, but Near Eastern and Canaanite-Egyptian influences were strong. The chief Philistine god, Dagon, was probably adopted from the Canaanites. As a god of crop fertility and natural renewal, Dagon was worshiped widely in the ancient Near East – his cult is known to go back to at least 2000 BCE. He is often depicted with the head and arms of a man and the tail of a fish. Dagon is also closely related to the Canaanite god Baal.

A Philistine temple site in use from 1150 to 1050 BCE has been excavated at Tell Qasile, just north of modern Tel Aviv and near the northern border of the Philistine lands. The deity worshiped here was probably not Dagon, but rather a variant of the Earth Mother goddess revered under different names throughout the Near East. Three temples have been found at this site, built one on top of the other. In the largest and latest of the temples, the ceiling of the main hall rested upon two pillars of cedar wood with ornamented limestone bases. Around the walls were stone benches coated in plaster. At the western end of the main hall was a raised altar, behind which lay a small room used to store offerings.

Many pottery vessels used in rituals have been unearthed here. Among these are incense burners and vases, some decorated with animal motifs. Female figurines have also been found, as well as pottery masks with human and animal faces. Finds of ash and animal bones suggest that worship at the temple involved animal sacrifices.

Third Tell Qasile Temple
This reconstruction (right) is based on the third temple at Tell Qasile, built in the 11th century BCE. The building was 14.5m (45 feet) long and 8m (25 feet) wide. The lower illustrations show the stages by which this temple developed on the site.

Philistine pottery (left). These figures are both in the typical style of Philistine work in clay. At the top is a large lid, made to be sealed on a clay coffin. It has stylized human features, including small arms folded across the chest. Below is a figurine of a fertility goddess from the second temple at Tell Qasile. It is 33cm (13 inches) tall and was probably used as a libation vessel, with the breasts acting as spouts.

The excavations at Tell Qasile (below) in 1980 uncovered a wide variety of goods, such as incense burners, jugs, bowls, and an iron bracelet. Animal bones found around the altar suggest that sheep, cattle, goats, and even a hippopotamus had been sacrificed to the goddess while the temple was in use.

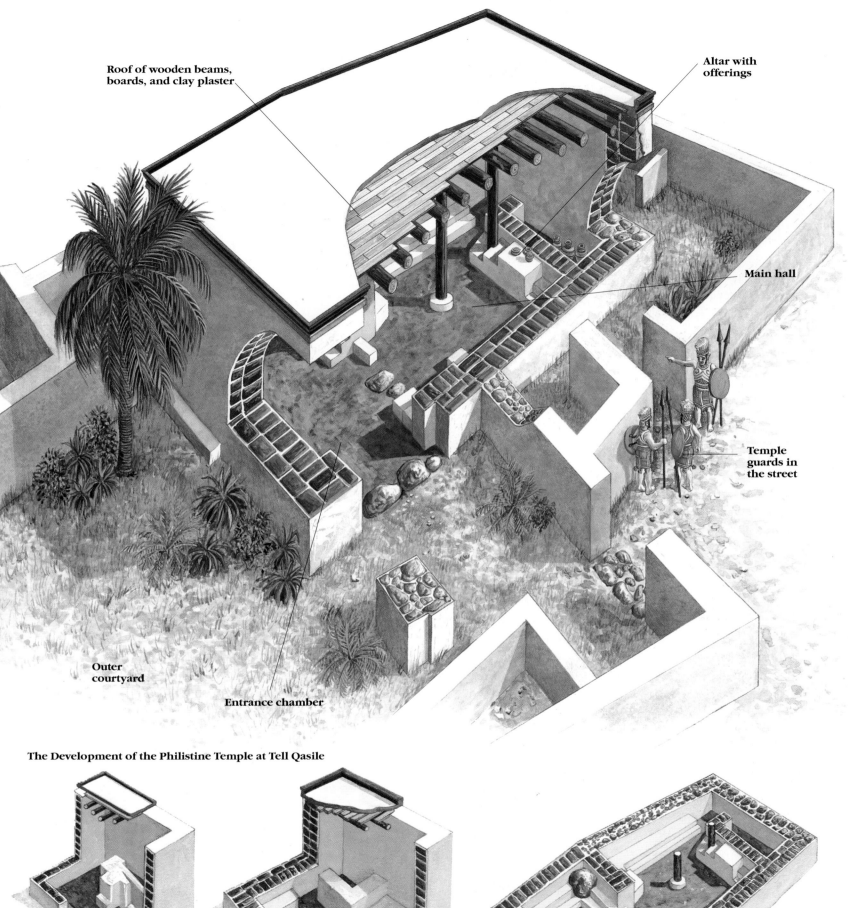

Roof of wooden beams, boards, and clay plaster

Altar with offerings

Main hall

Temple guards in the street

Outer courtyard

Entrance chamber

The Development of the Philistine Temple at Tell Qasile

First temple
(1150 BCE)

Second temple
(1100 BCE)

Third temple
(ground level)
(1050 BCE)

The growing strength of the Philistines in the coastal areas of Canaan soon led to conflict between Philistines and Israelites. The Israelite areas in the hilly regions to the north and west gradually fell under Philistine control. Although ordinary people of the two nations lived in neighboring communities, the Bible makes it clear that by the early 11th century BCE the Israelites

A highly decorated Philistine vase

had come to resent Philistine domination. But at last, the Bible says, God brought the Israelites a deliverer.

God told the barren wife of a man named Manoah that she would bear a son, who was to be brought up to follow the strictest of religious regimes; most importantly, his hair was never to be cut. The child was named Samson.

Samson and the lion

One day, when Samson had grown up, he saw a woman in the nearby Philistine town of Timnah whom he immediately

■ Coax him, and find out what makes his strength so great, and how we may overpower him ...

Judges 16:5

wished to marry. Returning to the town with his parents, Samson was attacked by a lion. Filled with the strength of God, he tore the lion apart with his bare hands. On his way home, he saw a swarm of bees and some honey within the lion's carcass, so he took some of the honey and ate it. He told no one about either incident.

Samson married his Philistine bride, and at the wedding feast he set the guests a riddle: 'Out of the eater came something to eat. Out of the strong came something sweet.' He promised 30 sets of clothes to anyone who could solve the riddle, demanding the same in return if they failed. Unable to work out the answer, the guests told Samson's wife that they would kill him if she did not find it out for them. Terrified, she coaxed the solution from Samson – it was a reference to

Carved lions fight ferociously in this basalt relief found in the Canaanite city of Beth-shean. The carving is now in a Jerusalem museum. The image of the lion was commonly used to represent great physical power and was an important symbol both in the Near East and Mycenean Greece, which heavily influenced the culture of the Philistines. The fact that Samson managed to kill a lion with his bare hands served to illustrate the magnitude of his God-given, superhuman strength.

*A **stone relief** (above) from the temple of Rameses III in Egypt shows Philistine soldiers, in their plumed helmets and tassled kilts, being taken prisoner by the Egyptians after the great Egyptian victory over the Sea Peoples in 1180 BCE. The Philistines were probably the strongest enemies faced by the Israelites in the period leading up to the unification of the Israelite kingdom under King David in 1000 BCE.*

the lion and the honey – and told the wedding guests. In fury, Samson killed 30 Philistine men, gave their clothes to the other guests, and left his new wife. He later tried to visit her, but her father would not let him. In vengeance, he set fire to the Philistines' fields of grain, vineyards, and olive groves. The Israelites, afraid of the consequences, handed Samson over to their overlords, but he escaped easily and killed a thousand Philistines using only the jawbone of a donkey as a weapon.

Samson and Delilah

Samson's strength became legendary, and he gained a great reputation as an unofficial military leader in the increasingly

The Philistines developed a distinctive style of pottery after they arrived in Canaan. This elegant beer jug (right) dates from the 12th century BCE, the period in which the Philistines settled Canaan. It is decorated in a very fluid, freehand style.

The Philistines in Canaan
The Philistines probably originated around the eastern Mediterranean and moved into Canaan during the migrations of the Sea Peoples. They dominated the southwest of Canaan from their five main cities of Ashdod, Ashkelon,

Ekron, Gath, and Gaza. As they encroached on neighboring lands, the Philistines soon inspired resentment and resistance among the Israelites. The stories of the deeds of Samson preserve much of the tension of the time.

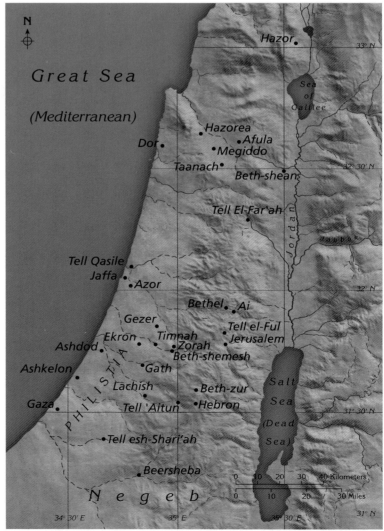

bitter struggle between the two peoples. Then he met another Philistine woman, who was to be his downfall.

Samson fell in love with Delilah, and the rulers of her city offered her a huge bribe to discover the secret of Samson's strength. Three times she asked him, and three times Samson deceived her. Finally her persistence paid off, and Samson revealed the true source of his power: his long, uncut hair. While he slept with his head in her lap, Delilah had his hair cut off. Without his braids Samson lost his superhuman strength; the Philistines seized him, bound him with ropes, and gouged out his eyes.

In celebration, the Philistines crowded into the temple of Dagon in Gaza to offer a great sacrifice. Samson was brought in to entertain them. He prayed fervently to God, pleading with him to restore his strength. Then he asked to be allowed to feel the two giant pillars which supported the temple roof. Bracing himself against them, he pushed with all his might. The temple collapsed, crushing both Samson and his captors.

Battle of Mount Gilboa in a medieval manuscript

The Israelites continued their conflict with the Philistines until they eventually suffered a severe blow at their hands: the capture of the Ark of the Covenant. The Ark was kept at the shrine at Shiloh under the protection of Eli the priest. Eli was a good man, but his sons were sinful and debauched. One night, Eli's young attendant Samuel heard the voice of God warning him of an impending disaster that would befall the Israelites as a punishment for the misdeeds of Eli's sons. Shortly after this, the Philistines won a great victory at Aphek, and so the Israelites decided to send the Ark of the Covenant into the next battle to bolster their confidence and improve their chances of victory. They collected the Ark from Shiloh, and it was borne into battle by Eli's sons. The Philistines were terrified, but the Israelites were still defeated. Eli's sons were killed in the battle, and the Ark was captured by the enemy.

The Ark, however, proved to be a liability to the Philistines. When it was taken to the temple of their god, Dagon, the idol fell down in front of it and shattered. No matter where they took the Ark, disaster followed it: the people developed tumors and their towns became overrun with mice. After seven months of suffering because of its presence, the Philistines, in desperation, returned the Ark to the Israelites.

Samuel becomes Judge and leader of Israel

By the time the Ark was restored, Eli the priest was dead, but his protégé, Samuel, took his place and grew up to be a Judge and leader of his people. Samuel led them well, but as conflict with the Philistines continued, the Israelites felt the need for a

> ■ Samuel took a vial of oil and poured it on [Saul's] head ... he said, 'The Lord has anointed you ruler over his people Israel.'
>
> 1 Samuel 10:1

stronger central authority, and began to clamor for a king. Samuel agreed and a search for a suitable candidate began.

The choice fell upon Saul, a man renowned for his bravery and great physical presence. Samuel anointed him king, and Saul soon took action against the Philistines, winning a spectacular victory at Michmash. Saul's whole reign was spent fighting against the enemies who threatened Israel from every side. Although he was a great warrior, Saul was not without faults; he disobeyed God and was subject to severe bouts of depression. Gradually, Samuel began to regret his choice and turned against Saul. Under God's instruction, Samuel secretly anointed David, a young shepherd from Bethlehem, as Saul's eventual successor. Samuel had nothing more to do with Saul and died quietly, some years later, mourned by all of Israel.

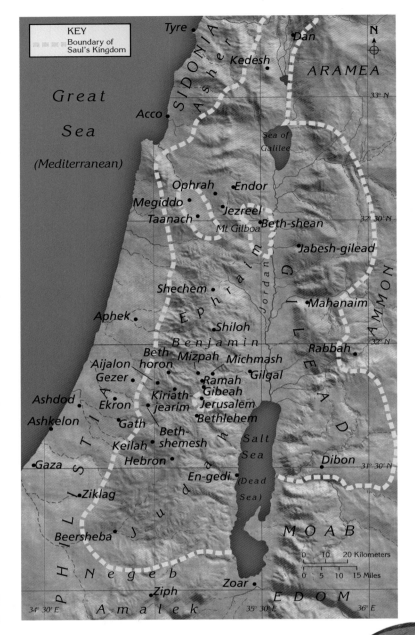

Saul's Kingdom
Saul emerged as the first king of Israel in around 1030 BCE. He was victorious in many battles against the Philistines as well as other warring tribes in Canaan. As the relative strengths of his own and his enemies' armies changed, so did the boundaries of his kingdom. This map shows the fullest extent of Saul's kingdom at the height of his military power.

Saul continued to oppose the Philistines, finally facing a huge army at Mount Gilboa. Before the battle Saul asked for God's advice, but the Lord did not answer him. Instead, Saul turned to the counsel of a medium, the witch of Endor, persuading her to conjure up the spirit of Samuel. The spirit castigated Saul, predicting disaster. At the battle, the Israelites suffered a shattering defeat and Saul fell on his own sword rather than be captured. The Philistines beheaded his body and strung it up. Later, the men of Jabesh-gilead, a city Saul had once saved from the enemy, took his body and buried it.

This rugged area *around Beth-horon (above and above right) is typical of the hill country on the edge of the Ephraimite mountains where much of the fighting between the Israelites and the Philistines took place. This terrain gave* *both sides opportunities to use guerilla tactics with ambushes and raids, and its caves and valleys also provided excellent refuges. From Michmash, the Philistines sent out raiding parties, one of which went along the Beth-horon road .*

The Battle of Michmash

The gorge at Michmash (right) was on a major Philistine route from the coast to the interior, and was the site of one of Saul's greatest victories. Saul's success was largely due to the surprise raid that his son Jonathan, together with his armorbearer, made on the Philistine forces, throwing them into confusion. The battle plan (above) shows (1) the route of Saul's army from Geba to Migron, (2) the Philistines' blocking force at the passage of Michmash, (3) Jonathan and his armorbearer's route from

Geba, (4) Jonathan's surprise attack of the blocking force, (5) Saul's frontal attack on the Philistines at Michmash, and (6) the Philistines' retreat.

Samuel chooses Saul to be king of the Israelites in this 13th-century fresco from the cathedral of Anagni, Italy. It shows the bearded Samuel, with a halo, offering food to Saul seated at the right of the table. Having previously met Saul in the street, Samuel invited him to stay the night at his house. The next day, as Saul was setting off on his journey home, Samuel took him to one side and anointed him with oil, telling him that he would be ruler of the people of Israel and would deliver them from their enemies.

David and Goliath depicted in a 13th-century manuscript

On God's instructions, the priest Samuel went to Bethlehem to anoint one of the sons of Jesse as King Saul's successor. Afraid that Saul would hear of this and be angry, Samuel kept his true purpose secret, merely asking Jesse and his family to join him for a sacrifice. Samuel met seven of Jesse's sons but recognized none of them as God's chosen. When Samuel asked if Jesse had any more sons he was told that the youngest boy, David, was out minding the sheep. David was sent for and on meeting him, Samuel realized immediately that this was the brother that God had chosen and anointed him.

David came to Saul's court and intitially found favor with the king. He soothed Saul's depressions with his singing and harp playing – tradition makes him the author of many of the Psalms. At this time, the Philistine champion, Goliath, a man over three metres tall and well armed, kept challenging the Israelites to produce an opponent to face him in single combat. None of the Israelites dared to respond except David, who offered to meet him. Saul agreed and David went out, armed only with a sling, to face Goliath's taunts. Using a smooth stone from the river as ammunition, David aimed straight for Goliath's forehead. The shot hit home and Goliath died instantly. David cut off Goliath's head and was hailed a

■ He chose his servant David ... to be the shepherd of his people Jacob, of Israel, his inheritance.

Psalm 78: 70–71

hero. He became close friends with the king's son, Jonathan, and also married one of his daughters. But Saul was jealous of David's popularity and tried to kill him. Fearing for his friend's life, Jonathan warned David of the danger, and he escaped.

Saul pursues David

Instead of fighting his Philistine enemies, Saul pursued David but as his men were closing in, Saul was called away to face a Philistine attack. David then escaped to En-gedi, a spring in the desert. When Saul resumed the chase, David and his men hid in a cave. While they were there Saul came in but didn't see them. David's men urged him to kill the king but David refused, secretly cutting off a corner of Saul's robe instead. David then followed Saul out of the cave and told him what had happened. Saul was full of remorse, and for a time they were reconciled. Nonetheless Saul's enmity persisted and again David showed his loyalty. One night David stole into Saul's camp but stopped short of killing his king, merely taking the spear and water jug from beside his bed as proof

that he had been there. On learning that David had again passed up a chance to kill him, Saul was once more filled with remorse. Despite this, David still feared him and sought refuge with Achish, a Philistine king. Achish wanted David to join him against Saul but the other Philistines objected, so David was not present at their eventual victory at Mount Gilboa, where both Saul and David's beloved friend Jonathan were killed.

This 4th-century mosaic pavement from the Basilica Aquileia in Italy shows a good shepherd with his sheep. The youthful David would have been just such a figure. The youngest of Jesse's eight sons, David was given the menial task of caring for his father's sheep. Like the shepherd pictured here with his panpipes, David too was musical. He played the lyre or harp and has been credited with writing many of the Psalms. He first came to Saul's court as a musician to soothe the king's moods with his playing.

Samuel anoints David as king of the Jews in this 3rd-century painting from the Dura-Europos Synagogue, Syria – now in the Damascus Museum. Samuel traveled to Bethlehem to find the new king among the sons of a man named Jesse. After meeting all eight sons he realized that it was David, the youngest, who was God's choice and Samuel anointed him there and then in front of his brothers.

David slew Goliath in the Valley of Elah (above). Saul and the Israelites were camped on a hill to one side of the valley, while the Philistines faced them from a hill on the other side. Both armies had an excellent view of the apparently unequal contest between the giant Philistine champion, Goliath, and the boy David. When they saw their champion slain by a shot from David's sling, the Philistines fled.

The spring at En-gedi (left) is situated in a barren area on the western shore of the Dead Sea, lying to the east of the Wilderness of Judah. This oasis is surrounded by mountains riddled with caves, and it was in one of these caves that David sought refuge from Saul and his troops. Saul had turned against David in jealousy after the young man's popularity grew following his victory over Goliath the Philistine.

Sling stone

The Deadly Sling

The sling, essentially a small catapult, was a commonly seen weapon in David's time. Shepherds would use slings to frighten off animal predators that might threaten their flock, so it is likely that David learned his skill with the sling when he was given charge of his father's sheep. Simple, light and portable, slings were made from a leather or cloth pouch with elongated edges or attached cords.

Stone projectiles, such as that shown above, were custom-made for use with a sling, although naturally occurring stones of the appropriate size, shape and weight were equally effective. The stone was put into the pouch, which was swung above the head and released, as shown in the Aramean stone relief, above left. In the hands of a skilled user the sling could be very accurate and required little strength to be effective. It was the perfect weapon for the slight, nimble David to use against the lumbering, heavily armored Goliath.

King David, as depicted in a 15th-century Book of Psalms

After the decisive battle at Mount Gilboa between the Israelites and the Philistines, where both King Ŝaul and his son Jonathan were killed, the mantle of kingship fell to David, son of Jesse. David had been anointed as Saul's successor some years previously and he went on to become Israel's greatest king and probable author of many of the Psalms. Yet initially, David inherited problems. The Philistines had acted quickly after their victory at Mount Gilboa and soon recovered all the lands they had earlier lost to the Israelites. Saul's other son, Ishbaal, fled across the Jordan and set up a government in exile to oppose David, who was based in Hebron. The rival houses split the Israelites and sparked a conflict that lasted several years.

This warfare gradually weakened Ishbaal's forces and after seven years he was murdered by his own men. David, now 30, became king over a united Israel and would reign until his death some 33 years later.

The capture of Jerusalem

David's first military act as king was to attack the city of Jerusalem, then a major Canaanite stronghold. His men found

■ The Rock of Israel has said to me: 'One who rules over people ... in the fear of God, is like the light of morning ...'

2 Samuel 23:3–4

a tunnel leading under the city walls from the Gihon Spring, the city's water supply, and used it to gain surprise entry. Jersualem fell without a fight and David made the city his capital – situated as it was on the frontier between Judah and the rest of Israel. He built a royal palace to mark his victory, and to great rejoicing, brought the Ark of the Covenant to Jerusalem after it had lain neglected for a generation. Its presence made David's capital the center of the nation's religious life, a symbol of divine blessing upon his reign.

Alarmed at David's new power, the Philistines mustered their forces but David defeated them completely. He went on to further military successes, extending his kingdom well to the east of the Jordan. In contrast to these victories, David's life at court was full of intrigue and tragedy. David had fallen in love with a beautiful woman he had seen bathing. She was Bathsheba, the wife of Uriah the Hittite, one of David's best soldiers. David sent for her and slept with her and she became pregnant. To hide his sin, David ensured that Uriah was killed in battle and he took Bathsheba for his wife. But his actions angered God and their child, a son, died. Bathsheba later gave David another son, Solomon, whom God would love.

Further troubles arose when Amnon, another son of David's, raped and then rejected Tamar, his half-sister. Tamar's full brother Absalom killed Amnon and fled, returning only to lead a revolt against his father. The revolt was crushed and Absalom was killed but David greatly mourned his loss.

David lived to a frail old age, surrounded by plots over the succession among his surviving sons. Swayed by Bathsheba's pleas, he eventually appointed their son Solomon as his heir.

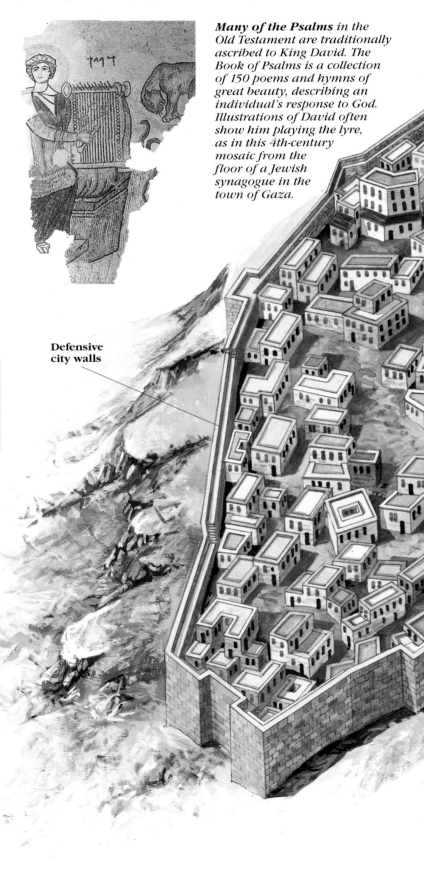

Many of the Psalms in the Old Testament are traditionally ascribed to King David. The Book of Psalms is a collection of 150 poems and hymns of great beauty, describing an individual's response to God. Illustrations of David often show him playing the lyre, as in this 4th-century mosaic from the floor of a Jewish synagogue in the town of Gaza.

Defensive city walls

David's palace

Position of shaft
to water supply

East or Water Gate

Gihon Spring

David's tower *is the oldest
surviving part of the Jerusalem
Citadel, which was built and
rebuilt several times on the site
of David's palace. This tower
dates from the time of Herod
the Great and now houses the
History of Jerusalem Museum.*

Jerusalem, the City of David
*There is little archeological
evidence of Jerusalem at the
time when the Bible says David
conquered the city, but its
weakest point, as David found
out, was the tunnel that
secured its water supply. This
ran from inside the city to the
water source, the Gihon Spring,
lying outside Jerusalem's walls.
The tunnel afforded David's
men access to the city without
having to assault its walls.*

Late-medieval view of the Judgment of Solomon

David died peacefully after a long and eventful reign, and the succession passed to his favored son Solomon. Not long after his accession, Solomon had a dream in which God told him to ask for whatever he wanted. Solomon admitted his inexperience and asked only for wisdom. Pleased with this answer, God promised him riches, honor, and long life.

Having inherited his father's empire, Solomon secured his position with a number of shrewd alliances, including marriage to the daughter of the Pharaoh of Egypt. In contrast to David's time, Solomon's reign was largely peaceful; the country flourished and traded widely.

Solomon began an ambitious building programme which included the Temple, a magnificent palace, and other official buildings. To defend his kingdom he fortified six cities and built up a standing army and a large force of war chariots.

■ 'Give your servant therefore an understanding mind to govern your people, able to discern between good and evil.'

1 Kings 3:9

The wisdom of Solomon

Although Solomon was famed for his great buildings, it was for his God-given wisdom that he gained a legendary reputation. He first displayed this judgment early in his reign when two women came to him, each claiming to be the mother of a new-born baby. To resolve the dispute, Solomon ordered the child to be cut in two and divided between them. In tears, one woman said she would rather her rival have the child than that it be killed. Solomon at once recognized her as the true mother, and gave her the child.

Solomon's knowledge extended into the realms of nature and philosophy, and the Old Testament books of Proverbs and Ecclesiastes are ascribed to him. News of his great learning reached the ears of the Queen of Sheba, and she decided to go to Jerusalem to test him for herself with difficult questions. He astounded her with his replies and duly satisfied, she

presented him with expensive gifts of gold, spices, and gems before returning home to Sheba.

Solomon is said to have had one flaw in the eyes of God. He took 700 wives and 300 concubines, many of them from foreign races, and allowed them to continue to worship pagan gods. Consequently he was not fully devoted to the Lord. Angry at this, God warned that after his death his sons would lose their inheritance and the kingdom would be divided.

A woman's head carved in stone from the land of Sheba. Although this dates from after Solomon's time, it has the word 'Sheba' inscribed on the headdress. After her visit to Solomon's court the Queen of Sheba was convinced of his wisdom.

Kiriath jearim
Ashkelon
PHILISTIA
Tama
EGYPT
Negeb
Valley of Sa
EDOM
KEY
Boundary of David's empire
Ezion-geber

These natural rock columns (left), standing in the Negeb Desert near ancient copper mines at Timnah, have been named 'Solomon's Pillars' as a reminder of the legendary 'King Solomon's Mines.' The Timnah copper workings predate Solomon, but ore was still mined here in his day, and might have been among the various commodities he traded around the Mediterranean.

Megiddo was the centerpiece of Solomon's military reforms. The city lay strategically on the main road linking Syria and Egypt and it was here that Solomon built a 'chariot city' to house the main body of his force of 1400 war chariots. Extensive Israelite remains can still be seen at Megiddo (left), although these may be later than Solomon, dating from King Ahab's time.

N

Arvad
Hamath
Tiphsah
Euphrates

Great Sea (Mediterranean)

Kadesh

ARAM
(SYRIA)

Sidon

ARAM-ZOBAH

Tyre

Tadmor

Megiddo
Beth-shean
Hazor
Sea of
Galilee
Jordan
Damascus

ARAM-DAMASCUS

Joppa
Lower
Shechem
aalath
Beth-horon
Gezer
Helam
Gibeon
Jabbok
Mahanaim
Gath
Timnah
Jericho
Hebron
Jerusalem
Rabbah
Beersheba
AMMON
Madaba

Salt Sea
(Dead Sea)

MOAB

0
0
60
25
50
120 Kilometers
75 Miles

David and Solomon's Land
The Kingdom of Israel reached the height of its power around 1000–930 BCE. The Bible tells how David united Judah and Israel, and then extended his influence north into Syria, east across the Jordan, and south to the Red Sea. Vassal states on the edge of the kingdom retained some independence but paid tributes to David and Solomon.

Ezion-geber
Solomon's legendary wealth was based on trade. With the help of Phoenician craftsmen supplied by his ally, Hiram I of Tyre, he built up a merchant fleet at a place called Ezion-geber. The ships traded down the Red Sea to Ophir and came back laden with gold and silver, rare woods, incense, jewels and ivory, and, for the king's amusement, monkeys. Excavations at Tell el-Kheleifeh uncovered a strongly built fort with administrative buildings which may be the remains of Ezion-geber. In the groundplan (right), the areas marked in black have been identified as part of this fort, although

recent dating suggests they are too young to be Solomon's buildings. These structures were later incorporated into a much larger fort shown in grey.

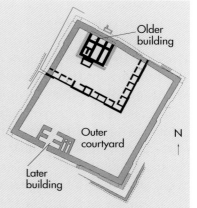

Older building

Outer courtyard

N

Later building

Ivory pomegranate thought to be from Solomon's temple

David wanted to build a temple to the glory of God but he was too preoccupied with war to do more than draw up the plans. David also amassed a great fortune to go toward the building of the temple, including 3500 tons of gold, a million talents of silver, and iron and bronze 'too great to be weighed.' In providing this wealth he remarked that he was only giving back to God what God had already given to him. David passed on his plans for the Temple to his son and successor, Solomon.

Work on the Temple began in the fourth year of Solomon's reign and took only seven years to complete. The site chosen was Mount Moriah, just north of the city of Jerusalem, where, according to Genesis, Abraham had prepared to sacrifice his son, Isaac.

Solomon relied heavily on Phoenician help to construct the Temple. His Phoenician ally, Hiram of Tyre, for instance, provided the finest cedar from Lebanon; the wood was floated down the coast to the ancient port of Joppa (Jaffa), and from there hauled overland to Jerusalem. Hiram also sent a skilled bronzesmith called Huram to supervise the extensive metal work in the Temple.

The design of the Temple reflected this Phoenician influence, although it also owed much to the layout of the

■ I have built you an exalted house, a place for you to dwell in forever ... Blessed be the Lord, the God of Israel ...

1 Kings 8:12–15

tabernacle – the portable sanctuary housing the Ark of the Covenant and the sacred tablets of the Law, which the Israelites had carried with them throughout their wanderings. The finished building was bigger than anything that the Jews had constructed before, although the palace that Solomon was later to build for himself was larger still.

The structure of the Temple

The Temple consisted of three areas: a vestibule or porch projecting in front of the main building; beyond this was a large rectangular chamber, called the Holy Place, which contained the altar and was lit by lamp standards; finally there was a small windowless cube, the Most Holy Place, which housed the Ark of the Covenant. This inner room was slightly raised above the Holy Place and approached from it by steps. The chambers were panelled with cedarwood so that no stonework was exposed inside the Temple. These panels were intricately decorated with carved and gilded patterns.

The Bible tells that when the Temple was finished, the priests carried the Ark of the Covenant into the Most Holy Place and placed it beneath a wood-and-gold canopy of

outspread cherubim wings, symbolizing God's protection. At that moment the glory of God filled the Temple in the form of a cloud. Solomon had thousands of beasts sacrificed during the Temple's consecration, a ceremony witnessed by a vast assembly including the elders and heads of the tribes of Israel.

Solomon's Temple must have inspired awe and wonder in all who approached it. Here, dominating Jerusalem, the capital of the Israelites, was a fit dwelling place for God, the creator of heaven and earth.

Cedars from Lebanon *were a valuable and much prized resource. Great forests of cedar covered the mountains of Lebanon in biblical times, but these have since dwindled to isolated groves as shown in the photograph above.*

Timber is transported by sea *in this Assyrian stone relief. The cut Lebanon cedar sent by Hiram of Tyre to Solomon to use in the construction of the Temple was transported in much this manner from Lebanon to Jaffa.*

Solomon's Temple
Although there is no archeological evidence for Solomon's Temple, the Bible gives a very detailed description of it from which this reconstruction was drawn. The Temple was built from cedar and stone and decorated inside with gold, silver, and ivory. A massive basin in front of the Temple was known as 'The Sea.'

'The Sea'

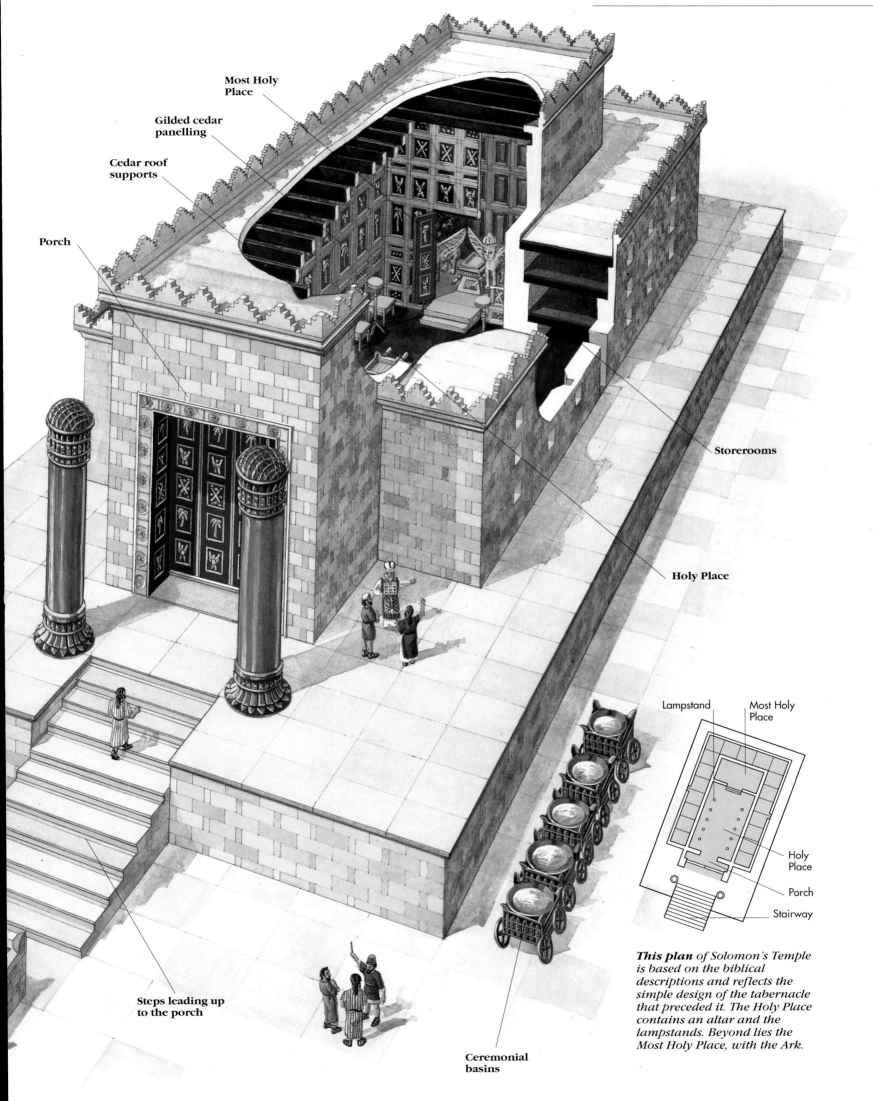

Most Holy
Place

Gilded cedar
panelling

Cedar roof
supports

Porch

Storerooms

Holy Place

Lampstand

Most Holy
Place

Holy
Place

Porch

Stairway

Steps leading up
to the porch

Ceremonial
basins

*This plan of Solomon's Temple
is based on the biblical
descriptions and reflects the
simple design of the tabernacle
that preceded it. The Holy Place
contains an altar and the
lampstands. Beyond lies the
Most Holy Place, with the Ark.*

Seal of Shema, a court official, from the time of Jeroboam II

Solomon's long reign was both peaceful and prosperous, but soon after his death, unrest and dissension that had been rumbling beneath the surface for some years erupted. The heavy taxes and forced labor needed to carry out some of Solomon's more grandiose schemes had caused serious disaffection within the country. In 930 BCE an assembly of the tribes of Israel came to Solomon's son and successor, Rehoboam, refusing to support him as the new king unless he lifted the burdens imposed by his father. Ignoring his advisers, Rehoboam dismissed their request so the northern tribes turned instead to Jeroboam, a former servant of Solomon's, to lead them.

In consequence, the kingdom was split in two. Israel in the north, led by Jeroboam, and Rehoboam's Judah in the south maintained an uneasy peace disrupted by occasional border skirmishes. With division came weakness; Judah was almost immediately plundered by the new Egyptian Pharaoh Shishak (or Shoshenq) I. This was soon followed by attacks from the

This wall relief *from Karnak (Thebes) in southern Egypt commemorates the plundering of Judah by the Pharaoh Shishak I in about 924 BCE. The Bible says that Shishak robbed the Temple of its treasures, and the relief lists 150 cities taken in the attack, including some in Israel. Rehoboam was unable to offer effective resistance, but in the end, unrest at home forced the invaders to withdraw.*

> ■ He then said to Jeroboam, ... 'See, I am about to tear the kingdom from the hand of Solomon, and will give you ten tribes.'
>
> I Kings 11:31

Arameans of Damascus, while the Philistines in the south and the Moabites and Ammonites to the east of the Jordan all regained their independence.

Decline and recovery of Israel and Judah

In the mid-9th century BCE, Assyria too began to assert its power. For 50 years its armies made sorties against Israel. Their attacks paved the way for the king of Damascus, Hazael, to capture the whole area of Transjordan as far south as Moab, reducing Israel to a puppet state. This is the period of the prophet Elisha, who ministered in the northern kingdom, performing miracles and acting as adviser to Israel's leaders.

Early in the 8th century BCE the balance of power swung back again when the king of Assyria crushed Damascus and imposed a heavy financial tribute. Israel was also forced to pay but was spared attack. Then King Joash (or Jehoash) began to have some successes against the Assyrians. His victories were built on by his son Jeroboam II, who extended Israel's borders almost as far as they had been in David's day.

Judah fared little better than Israel during this time. It had suffered economically from the loss of Israel's fertile land, and was weakened by conflict with its neighbors. Its people had turned to paganism and only when King Uzziah (783–42 BCE), revived the worship of God did Judah's fortunes revive.

The Divided Kingdom
Neither David nor Solomon was ever able completely to resolve the longstanding differences between the tribes of the north and those of the south. In c.930 BCE, following Solomon's death, the situation came to a head with the secession of the northern kingdom of Israel from the southern kingdom of Judah. Jeroboam of Israel established his capital at Shechem, while Judah's government, under Rehoboam, remained in Jerusalem. The border between the two kingdoms was constantly subject to skirmishes.

KEY
- - - - - Boundary between
Israel and Judah

Great Sea
(Mediterranean)

Sidon

Tyre

Dan

Damascus

Kedesh

Hazor

S I D O N I A

A R A M -
D A M A S C U S

Dor

Sea
of
Galilee

GESHUR

Megiddo

Beth-shean

Samaria

Shechem

I S R A E L

Joppa

Aphek

Tirzah

Ramoth-gilead

Shiloh

Jordan

Ashdod

Beth-horon

Bethel

Jabbok

Penuel

Ashkelon

Gezer

Jericho

Mahanaim

Gath

Jerusalem

A M M O N

Hebron

Tekoa

Salt

Rabbah

Arad

Sea
(Dead
Sea)

Arnon

Dibon

M O A B

Mizpah *was one of the towns on the border between the divided kingdoms of Judah and Israel. It lay just inside Judah, while its neighboring city of Ramah was in Israel. Mizpah provides evidence of the bitter internal wrangling that tore the divided kingdom ever further apart. The town was fortified around 900 BCE by Rehoboam's grandson, Asa, king of Judah, against attacks from the north. This aerial photograph shows the ruins of the old fortified city in the center, surrounded by modern buildings and roads.*

Elijah the Prophet

Following Solomon's death and the consequent division of the kingdom into Israel in the north and Judah in the south, Israel's link with Jerusalem was broken. As a result, there was a resurgence of the pagan cults of Canaan among the people of the north. Jezebel, the wife of Israel's King Ahab (873–853 BCE), for instance, promoted the worship of Baal, and a temple to Baal was built at Samaria, the new capital of the north.

Ahab's chief opponent was the prophet Elijah, a wild-looking man from Tishbe in Gilead. Elijah warned of a prolonged drought but Ahab ignored him. With God's help Elijah survived the drought, being fed by ravens, and then being cared for by a poor widow whom God miraculously kept provided with flour and oil.

After three years of drought, Elijah challenged the priests of Baal to a test on Mount Carmel to prove their god's power: each side was to prepare a sacrifice, and the true god would send down fire to burn the sacrifice. The priests of Baal danced and called to their god, but to no avail. Then Elijah prayed to the Lord and at once fire consumed his offering. The people were terrified and on Elijah's orders they slaughtered the priests of Baal, much to Jezebel's fury. Very soon, heavy rain began to fall.

In fear of Jezebel's anger Elijah fled south to Mount Horeb – now Sinai. There God spoke to him in a gentle whisper, telling him to go back and anoint a new king, Jehu, together with Elisha who would be his successor as prophet. After Ahab died in battle, Jehu eventually assumed power and systematically eradicated Baal's supporters. Jezebel herself was thrown from a window and her body was trampled by horses and eaten by dogs.

The prophet Elijah did not die. He was talking with Elisha one day when a fiery chariot swept him up to heaven. In Jewish tradition, he is expected to return as forerunner of the Messiah. The New Testament regards John the Baptist as the reincarnation of Elijah.

Above: Byzantine painting of Elijah being taken to heaven.
Background: Mount Horeb in the desert of Sinai.
Map: The extent of Ahab and Jezebel's kingdom.

1. Mount Carmel.
2. Synagogue painting of the priests of Baal on Mount Carmel.
3. Bronze frieze of an Assyrian victory over King Jehu.
4. Ivory carving from Ahab's time.

33·2565

3

4

8th-century BCE ivory sphinx from Assyria

By the mid-8th century BCE Israel and Judah had regained most of the territory lost since the time of Solomon's empire. This meant that once again the two kingdoms controlled lucrative trade routes, and their prosperity grew accordingly. Yet, in the eyes of the prophet Amos, this prosperity itself brought new dangers.

Amos was a shepherd from the southern kingdom of Judah. God told him to go north to Israel and prophesy at the royal shrine of Bethel. There Amos attacked the immorality and luxury which were undermining the national character of Israel. He denounced the way that the rich oppressed the poor and warned of impending doom.

Decline of Israel

Amos' words forewarned of the imminent decline of Israel and its assimilation into the Assyrian empire, a rapidly growing Mesopotamian power to the northeast. Israel's troubles began after the death of King Jeroboam around 748 BCE. A rapid succession of weak kings followed, leaving

■ Therefore I will make Samaria a heap in the open country, a place for planting vineyards ... All her images shall be beaten to pieces.
Micah 1:6–7

the country ill-prepared to face the growing power of Assyria under its new and ambitious ruler, Tiglath-pileser III.

At first Israel bought peace with the Assyrians, but in 735 BCE Israel's King Pekah decided to change tactics. He tried to form alliances with neighboring states, including Judah, to oppose Tiglath-pileser. King Ahaz of Judah, however, refused

to join the alliance so Pekah began a military campaign against him. In response, Ahaz called on the help of Tiglath-pileser.

Needing no further excuse, the Assyrians invaded first Syria then Israel. They destroyed Damascus in 732 BCE and proceeded to sack the cities of Megiddo and Hazor. Within Israel, only the region of Samaria was temporarily spared when Israel's new king, Hoshea – who had murdered Pekah and seized the throne – decided to buy off the Assyrians with a generous tribute.

Sargon II, king of Assyria from 722 to 705 BCE, shown in a bas-relief (above) from his palace Dur-Sharukkin at Khorsabad, Iraq. He is talking to a high dignitary (the figure on the right), possibly the crown prince Sennacherib. Biblical details of Sargon's campaign in Samaria and the numbers of Israelite captives taken are confirmed by a surviving Assyrian victory inscription dating from his time.

Assyrian footsoldiers *from the time of Tiglath-pileser III and Sargon II, as shown in a bas-relief from northern Syria. These men are lightly armed*

troops, equipped with bows but no body armor. The Assyrians were noted for their savagery and ruthlessness in battle during this period.

Assyrian Expansion
In the late 8th century BCE the attitude of the powerful Assyrian kingdom toward the states on its borders became increasingly aggressive, leading eventually to the creation of what has been called the Neo-Assyrian empire. Under King Tiglath-pileser III and his successors, the Assyrians began to conquer and annex their neighboring kingdoms, rather than simply demand tributes from them. In 732 BCE, Syria and the kingdom of Israel were overrun. Samaria, the only part of Israel initially to be spared, was finally conquered by Sargon II in 722 BCE. He went on to deport large numbers of Israelites to Mesopotamia and brought immigrants from other parts of the Assyrian empire to settle in Israel.

The destruction of Israel

Israel's respite from Assyrian attention was short-lived. After the death of Tiglath-pileser in 727 BCE, Hoshea appealed unsuccessfully to Egypt for help. When Tiglath-pileser's son and successor, Shalmaneser V, discovered Hoshea's treachery he launched an attack against Israel. Hoshea was imprisoned and Samaria was occupied. The city of Samaria itself fell late in the summer of 722 BCE, probably to Shalmaneser's brother, Sargon II. Many of Israel's citizens were deported to Mesopotamia – some 27,290 according to surviving Assyrian records – and people were brought in from Babylon and other parts of the Assyrian empire to settle in Samaria and other northern towns. As a result, many inhabitants of the former kingdom of Israel were pagans, and not of Israelite descent.

According to the Book of Kings, this disaster was clearly a consequence of Israel's disobedience and unfaithfulness. Assyria's destruction of the kingdom of Israel was God's way of showing his anger at his people.

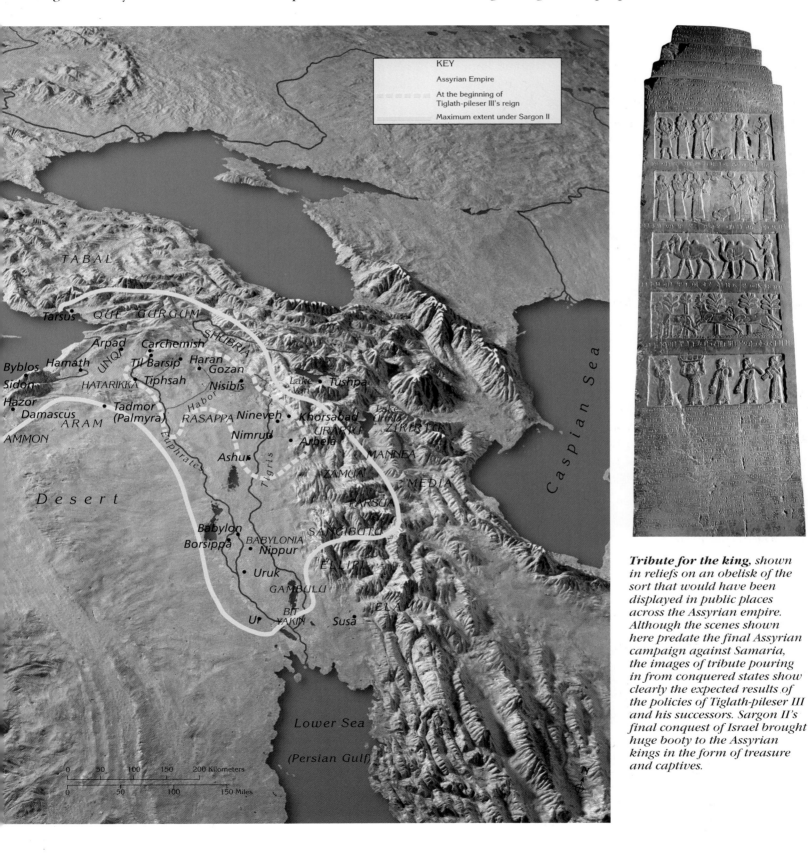

KEY

Assyrian Empire

At the beginning of
Tiglath-pileser III's reign

Maximum extent under Sargon II

Tribute for the king, shown in reliefs on an obelisk of the sort that would have been displayed in public places across the Assyrian empire. Although the scenes shown here predate the final Assyrian campaign against Samaria, the images of tribute pouring in from conquered states show clearly the expected results of the policies of Tiglath-pileser III and his successors. Sargon II's final conquest of Israel brought huge booty to the Assyrian kings in the form of treasure and captives.

A prophet carrying a Torah roll

The gradual subjugation of the northern kingdom of Israel by the Assyrians was regarded with increasing alarm by Judah. The prophet Micah warned that the destruction visited on Israel would inevitably be extended southward to Judah, and eventually, to the holy city of Jerusalem itself.

Under King Ahaz (735–715 BCE) Judah became a vassal state of the Assyrians and as such was required pay them tribute; Ahaz was also forced to set up an altar to Assyrian gods in the Temple in Jerusalem. The prophet Isaiah attacked this sacrilege and warned the people of the dangers of such faithlessness. Ahaz's successor, Hezekiah (715–687 BCE), took note of the prophet's warnings. He introduced many reforms aimed at restoring the purity of the Jewish religion – but he also sought to free Judah from the yoke of Assyrian rule.

In 705 BCE the powerful Assyrian ruler Sargon II died and was succeeded by his son Sennacherib, who immediately faced a major rebellion in Babylon, in the east of his empire.

Hezekiah grasped the opportunity, while Sennacherib was distracted, to stop the payment of tribute. With the backing of Egypt and of the Babylonian rebels, he formed a wide-ranging coalition of local kings prepared to oppose Assyrian rule.

Hezekiah prepares for war

Hezekiah undertook an extensive program of military preparations, funded by profits from trade he had initiated with Egypt and the Middle East. He refortified the most important citadels in his kingdom and restocked their arsenals with new weapons. Some Philistine strongholds had refused to join Hezekiah's coalition so he sent Judean troops to occupy these centers while he and his allies systematically deposed pro-Assyrian rulers in the region.

Marching past palm trees, *these Assyrian bowmen on parade (left) are members of an elite unit. They are wearing armor and characteristic Assyrian pointed helmets. Bowmen were among the most important and numerous troops in the Assyrian army.*

■ [Hezekiah] trusted in the Lord ... He rebelled against the king of Assyria and would not serve him.

2 Kings 18:5–7

An Assyrian bowman, *mounted on a galloping horse, prepares to release an arrow. This bas-relief actually shows the Assyrian king Ashurbanipal* *hunting, but he is fully equipped as if for war. The image illustrates the speed and power of the military force available to the Assyrians.*

In Jerusalem, Hezekiah strengthened the city walls and undertook the project for which he is best remembered – the construction of a tunnel – known ever since as 'Hezekiah's Tunnel' – to secure the city's water supply in time of siege.

Hezekiah himself fell ill during these preparations, but the prophet Isaiah offered assurances that he would recover and live for a further 15 years. All was prepared for Judah to face Assyria. Finally, in 701 BCE, Sennacherib attacked. A fierce Assyrian campaign in Phoenicia, north of the Philistine lands, prompted many members of the rebel coalition to sue for peace. But Judah and the Philistine cities of Ashkelon and Ekron held out. Sennacherib captured the two Philistine strongholds and executed or deported their inhabitants. He then advanced on the Judean fortress of Lachish.

Securing Jerusalem's Water

This plan of Jerusalem shows how Hezekiah's Tunnel brought water from the Gihon Spring, which lay outside the city wall, to the Siloam Pool, a reservoir inside the city. Earlier, the Siloam Pool had also lain outside the city walls, but it had been enclosed within the city by the large-scale extension of the wall also undertaken by Hezekiah. The original feeder channel for the reservoir, the Siloam Channel, was also outside the city wall and therefore vulnerable to attack. Hezekiah's Tunnel solved this problem by feeding water directly under the city wall, from the spring to the Siloam Pool, thereby ensuring a safe supply in times of siege.

Inscription on a rock found near the southern end of Hezekiah's Tunnel and the Siloam Pool. It describes the construction of the tunnel in Hezekiah's time, detailing the meeting of two teams of miners working from opposite ends.

The northern entrance to Hezekiah's Tunnel, which can still be seen today. The tunnel's winding path, running roughly parallel along much of its length to both the city wall and the Siloam Channel, followed a natural stratum of soft rock lying beneath the city. This made the tunnel relatively easy to excavate and may explain its sinuous route, as the miners followed the path of least resistance through the rock.

Jerusalem's Water Supply

The drawing below shows the various tunnels and shafts excavated over the centuries to access Jerusalem's main water supply – the Gihon Spring – which lay outside the city wall. Water was originally drawn from a shaft or well which is now known as Warren's Shaft, after the archeologist who discovered it. A stepped tunnel led to this shaft, at the bottom of which lay a pool fed by the spring. By Hezekiah's time this shaft was blocked. He therefore had a new tunnel dug to carry water inside the city to the Siloam Pool reservoir. Also illustrated is a later medieval access to the spring.

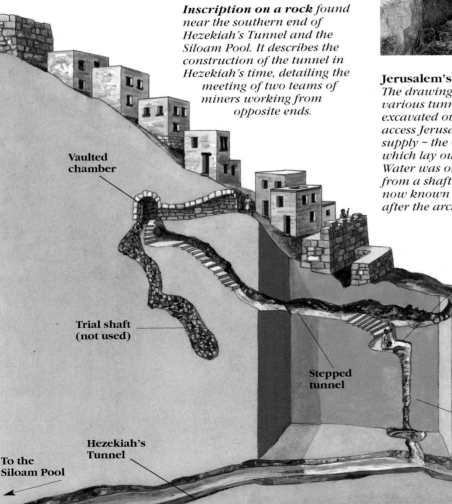

Vaulted chamber

Trial shaft (not used)

Water drawn from this platform

Guardhouse and access (medieval)

Stepped tunnel

Warren's Shaft

To the Siloam Pool

Hezekiah's Tunnel

Gihon Spring

The Battle for Lachish

In 701 BCE, the kingdom of Judah felt the full force of the invading Assyrian army of King Sennacherib. The Assyrians had already swept through Phoenicia, and gone on to seize the Philistine cities of Ashkelon and Ekron, at that time Judah's allies. Now Sennacherib turned his attention towards Judah itself. After victories at the cities of Azekah and Gath, he approached Lachish. Well fortified with thick inner and outer walls and strongly protected gates, the citadel of Lachish was regarded as a key stronghold. It was built on a steep-sided mound and consisted of two main areas: the royal sector, containing a high-walled compound, in which stood the great palace-fort; and, surrounding this, the rest of the city itself.

A set of amulets from 8th-century BCE Lachish

A large wall relief from Sennacherib's palace in Nineveh offers a dramatic view of the siege of Lachish. Its detail and immediacy suggest it was based on contemporary sketches. In it, defenders shoot arrows and hurl stones and flaming torches from towers along the outer wall. The Assyrians use siege engines equipped with battering rams to break down the walls. These are manned by a crew of three to guide and protect the ram. The relief also shows prisoners being led away, and the bodies of others impaled on stakes.

Despite the city's powerful defences and the determined efforts of its defenders, the Assyrians forced their way into Lachish. Many inhabitants were killed, but most were taken as prisoners before the Assyrians finally razed the city.

> ■ Do not be afraid ... before the king of Assyria and all the horde that is with him; for there is one greater with us than with him.
>
> 2 Chronicles 32:6

The salvation of Jerusalem

Encouraged by this decisive victory, Sennacherib sent a unit of men from Lachish directly to Jerusalem. As the Assyrians advanced on his capital, Judah's King Hezekiah tried to sue for peace. Sennacherib demanded an enormous tribute which the Judeans could meet only by stripping the gold from the Temple. To reinforce this demand, Sennacherib's commander Rabshakeh moved his large army up to the walls of Jerusalem and demanded its surrender. The situation was desperate. According to the Bible, Hezekiah put on sackcloth, went to the Temple, and prayed to God to save the city.

That night, the Bible says, an angel of God killed thousands of Assyrian soldiers. In response, Sennacherib decided to accept the tribute and reduce Judean territory, but to spare Jerusalem. He withdrew his army and returned home, where he was assassinated soon afterwards by his own sons. In contrast, Hezekiah, savior of Jerusalem, reigned peacefully in his reduced kingdom for another 15 years.

The siege of Lachish, as shown in the Lachish Reliefs, which were discovered in the 19th century in the remains of Sennacherib's palace at Nineveh, Iraq. The general view of part of Slabs 2 and 3 (above) shows Assyrian siege engines supported by archers and spearmen advancing up the siege ramp against the walls. Stones, firebrands, and other missiles (including part of a siege ladder) rain down on the besiegers. One member of the crew of the battering ram in the center pours water over it to prevent it from being set alight by the firebrands thrown by the defenders. Many of the details shown in the reliefs have been confirmed by archeological exploration at the site of Lachish itself.

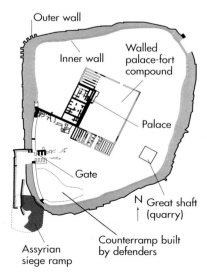

Lachish during the siege (left). The city was built on a steep-sided hill, and could only be approached from the southwest corner, near the main gate – so it was here that the besiegers built a huge ramp to give their siege engines access to the walls. Using stone and rubble excavated from the quarry now known as the 'great shaft,' the defenders built their own counterramp to reinforce the inner wall and to allow as many men as possible to shoot arrows and hurl missiles at the attacking forces.

Outer wall
Inner wall
Walled palace-fort compound
Palace
Gate
N Great shaft (quarry)
Counterramp built by defenders
Assyrian siege ramp

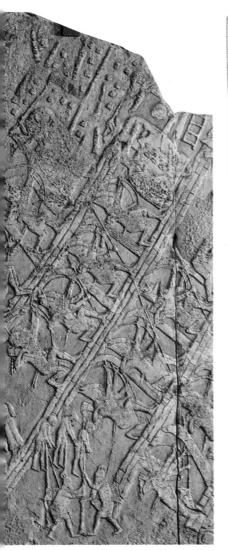

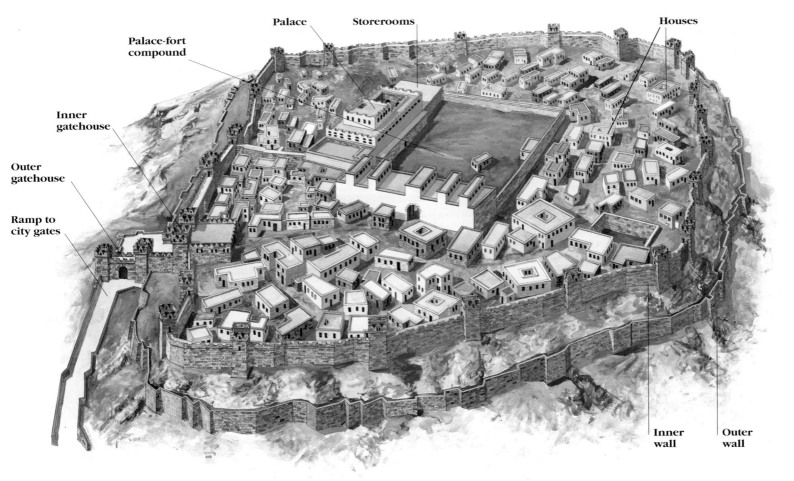

The Prism of Sennacherib
*(above), made of baked clay,
details in Assyrian cuneiform
script the king's annals,
including his third campaign
in Judah in 701 BCE, leading to
the siege and sack of Lachish.*

Judah and Philistia in 701 BCE
*The Israelite kingdom of Judah
faced dangerous neighbors to
the north and to the west in the
late 8th century BCE. Jerusalem
guarded the northern frontier,
facing the Assyrian-occupied
former kingdom of Israel,
while Lachish was the most
important stronghold on the*
*border with the lands of the
Philistines. After the Assyrian
army under Sennacherib had
reconquered the rebel Philistine
cities in early 701 BCE, Lachish
lay in its line of advance
against King Hezekiah of
Judah, who had encouraged
and supported the rebellion.*

The City of Lachish
*This reconstruction shows
Lachish as it would have been
on the eve of Sennacherib's
attack. At this time, Lachish
was probably the second most*
*important city in Judah after
Jerusalem. The large palace-fort
complex, and the two powerful
gatehouses with bronze-bound
wooden doors, indicate that the*
*city was a government center
and a military citadel, but the
congested residential areas
show that it was also home to
many ordinary citizens.*

Palace
Storerooms
Houses
Palace-fort
compound
Inner
gatehouse
Outer
gatehouse
Ramp to
city gates
Inner
wall
Outer
wall

Ezekiel's parable of Jerusalem's fall

The century following the death of King Hezekiah in 687 BCE saw the kingdom of Judah increasingly embroiled in the power struggles of its larger neighbors. Assyria was now at the height of its power, and a new threat was arising in Babylon to the east. Hezekiah's son Manasseh tried to ally Judah with the Phoenician cities of Tyre and Sidon, but offended his people by promoting the worship of Phoenician gods.

As Assyrian power waned, Judah temporarily reasserted its independence under Josiah (640–609 BCE), who also made religious reforms, reversing the policies of Manasseh. When his High Priest discovered 'The Book of the Law' – thought to be a version of the Book of Deuteronomy – Josiah pledged himself to follow God's way. Nonetheless, he was warned by a prophetess that his faith was not enough and that God intended to bring disaster upon the nation after his death.

Toward the end of the 7th century BCE the balance of power in the region changed. In 612 BCE the Babylonians and Medes, under the Babylonian ruler Nebuchadnezzar, captured and destroyed the Assyrian capital, Nineveh. The Egyptian

Hezekiah's wall, destroyed in the Babylonian sack of the city. Hezekiah's improved defenses had helped protect Jerusalem during the Assyrian assault, but failed to withstand siege by Babylon a century later.

Iron arrowheads dating from the time of Nebuchadnezzar's siege of Jerusalem, found at the foot of a tower in the city wall. Bows and arrows were the most important missile weapons in both armies.

The Babylonian Empire
As the empire of the Assyrians declined in the late 7th century BCE, its powerful eastern rival, Babylon, grew in strength. The kingdom of Judah was caught up in the struggle between the two, and in Egypt's attempts to intervene. The Babylonians

defeated the Assyrians, drove out the Egyptians, and created a vast new empire. They twice invaded Judah, annexing the Israelite kingdom. After the sack of Jerusalem in 586 BCE, they carried off its leading citizens into exile in Babylon.

LYDIA

HATTI-LAND

Kirshu

Carchemish

Qurama

CYPRUS

Arvad

Kadesh
Hamath

Orontes

Riblah

N

Sidon
Tyre

SYRIA

Great Sea (Mediterranean)

Damascus

Dor

Sea of Galilee

Megiddo

SAMARIA

Jordan

Gezer
Ekron

Mizpah

AMMON

Ashkelon
Gaza

Jerusalem

Lachish

JUDAH

Salt Sea (Dead Sea)

EDOM

Memphis

Nile

EGYPT

SINAI

Red Sea

KEY
Extent of Babylonian Empire
Route into exile

God's punishment of Israel – a 3rd-century painting (left) of Ezekiel's vision, from Dura-Europos, Syria. Deported to Babylon after the defeat of Judah, the prophet Ezekiel foresaw the final destruction of Jerusalem in 586 BCE.

Part of a letter in Hebrew inscribed on a fragment of pottery (right) found at Lachish. It relates to the siege of the city by Nebuchadnezzar during Judah's struggle against the Babylonians in 589 BCE.

Pharaoh Neco II set out to support the Assyrians. Josiah intervened against him, but was killed in battle at Megiddo.

Neco demanded a heavy tribute from Judah and installed Jehoiakim as a puppet ruler. In 605 BCE, the Babylonians defeated the Egyptians and in 598 BCE they invaded Judah. The following year, on 16 March, Jerusalem surrendered, as the prophet Jeremiah had foreseen. The leading citizens were taken as captives; among them was the prophet Ezekiel, who warned that Jerusalem would soon be completely destroyed.

Nebuchadnezzar appointed another puppet king, Zedekiah, but when he rebelled in 589 BCE, the full might of the Babylonian army again descended on Judah. Jerusalem was besieged for over a year and its inhabitants reduced to starvation. When the city wall was finally breached, in July 586 BCE, the Temple was destroyed and the city was sacked, looted, and burned. Zedekiah was captured; his sons were killed, and he was blinded. Zedekiah and all but the poorest people of the city were taken into exile in Babylon.

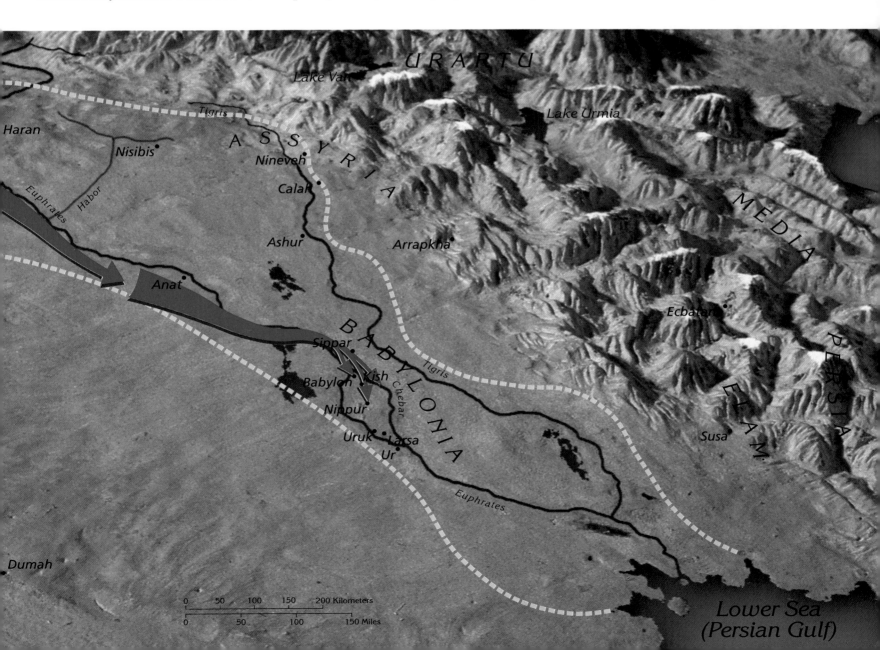

Decorated wall in the palace throne-room

The destruction of Jerusalem and its Temple by the Babylonians, and the enforced journey into Babylonia of the exiled Jews, left them feeling that they had been abandoned by God. But the prophets Jeremiah and Ezekiel assured them that they, God's children, would eventually return with renewed faith to the Promised Land.

According to the Book of Jeremiah, 4600 Jews were deported, but this may refer only to adult males, and the total number, including women and children, could have been thousands more. Significantly, these exiles included the country's political and religious elite, their departure leaving their homeland bereft of leadership.

The city they came to, Babylon, was then the largest in the world. It was laid out in a grid pattern with thriving wharves along the River Euphrates. Dominating the city was the great temple of Marduk with its ancient ziggurat. The Jewish exiles, however, regarded Babylon as a city of vice. The Book of Daniel tells how when Babylon's king, Nebuchadnezzar, boasted about building this great city, he was afflicted with a madness sent by God. He was driven away to live as a beast among wild animals until he acknowledged the dominion of the Lord. Only then was his sanity restored.

Jewish life in exile

The Jewish exiles were placed in special settlements in southern Mesopotamia, not far from Babylon, and were given considerable freedom to organize themselves, and to earn their livings. It was probably at this time that the synagogue developed as a center for study, possibly as a substitute for the

■ By the rivers of Babylon – there we sat down and there we wept when we remembered Zion.

Psalm 137:1

Temple in Jerusalem. Some of the exiles, including King Jehoiachin, may have achieved honors and high positions at the Babylonian court. The people were certainly influenced by their new surroundings. They adopted the Aramaic language, and may have borrowed ideas – such as a belief in Satan and in life after death – from Babylonian religions, particularly Zoroastrianism.

Despite their isolation, the prophet Jeremiah insisted that the future of the Jewish people lay with these exiles. He predicted that Babylon and its king would be destroyed, and that God would bring back his displaced people, making a new covenant with them. The message of Ezekiel, the priest and prophet, was the same: God would ensure the exiles' return and their faith would revive the 'dead bones' of Israel.

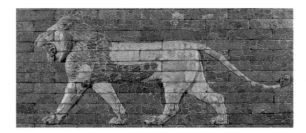

Ziggurat of Marduk or temple tower

Temple of Marduk

Temple of Ishtar

Temple of Ninmah

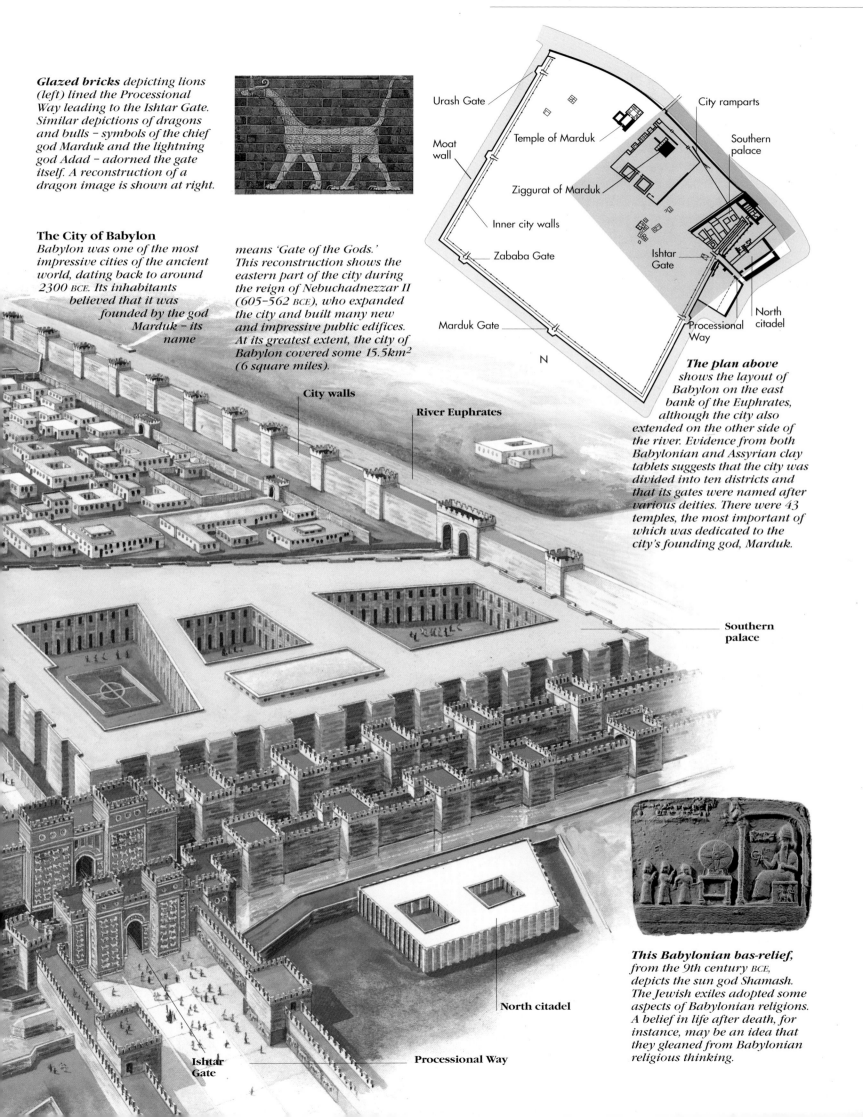

Glazed bricks depicting lions (left) lined the Processional Way leading to the Ishtar Gate. Similar depictions of dragons and bulls – symbols of the chief god Marduk and the lightning god Adad – adorned the gate itself. A reconstruction of a dragon image is shown at right.

The City of Babylon

Babylon was one of the most impressive cities of the ancient world, dating back to around 2300 BCE. Its inhabitants believed that it was founded by the god Marduk – its name means 'Gate of the Gods.' *This reconstruction shows the eastern part of the city during the reign of Nebuchadnezzar II (605–562 BCE), who expanded the city and built many new and impressive public edifices. At its greatest extent, the city of Babylon covered some 15.5km² (6 square miles).*

Urash Gate

Moat wall

Temple of Marduk

Ziggurat of Marduk

Inner city walls

Zababa Gate

Marduk Gate

City ramparts

Southern palace

Ishtar Gate

North citadel

Processional Way

N

The plan above shows the layout of Babylon on the east bank of the Euphrates, although the city also extended on the other side of the river. Evidence from both Babylonian and Assyrian clay tablets suggests that the city was divided into ten districts and that its gates were named after various deities. There were 43 temples, the most important of which was dedicated to the city's founding god, Marduk.

City walls

River Euphrates

Southern palace

North citadel

Ishtar Gate

Processional Way

This Babylonian bas-relief, from the 9th century BCE, depicts the sun god Shamash. The Jewish exiles adopted some aspects of Babylonian religions. A belief in life after death, for instance, may be an idea that they gleaned from Babylonian religious thinking.

Following Nebuchadnezzar's death in 562 BCE, the power of Babylon declined. His successor, Nabonidus, moved his court to Tema in the Arabian desert, leaving the city in the hands of his crown prince Bel-shar-usur (Belshazzar). According to the Book of Daniel, an astonishing event predicted Babylon's fall. One day, at a great feast, Belshazzar saw a disembodied hand writing on the wall. Nobody could interpret the message until Daniel, then a young Jewish courtier, was summoned. He read out the Aramaic words, *mene, mene, tekel, parsin*, explaining that they foretold the end of Belshazzar's reign and the imminent fall and division of Babylon.

Glazed brick frieze from Susa showing an armed guard

At this time a new power in the area was emerging – the Achemenid dynasty of Persia. Its rise began in 550 BCE with the accession of Cyrus the Great who crushed the empire of the Medes and swallowed up the great wealth of the Lydians.

Cyrus' crowning achievement came in 539 BCE when his army conquered the Babylonian forces. As a result, Babylon surrendered without resistance. Cyrus was hailed as a liberator and entered the city in triumph. He immediately began a policy of repatriation, freeing the exiled Jews and Babylon's other subject peoples, allowing them to return

■ Fallen, fallen is Babylon; and all the images of her gods lie shattered on the ground.

Isaiah 21:9

home. Within a year Cyrus had issued a decree restoring the treasures plundered by Nebuchadnezzar from the Temple in Jerusalem. Cyrus was widely regarded as a wise and tolerant ruler; in Isaiah he is even referred to as the Lord's anointed.

Cyrus' empire was later extended by his son Cambyses, who took Egypt in *c.*525 BCE. His successor, Darius the Great (521–486 BCE), was one of the most able of the Persian kings. Darius built himself a magnificent new capital at Persepolis to complement his administrative capital at Susa.

The Book of Daniel, which was written some 300 years after these events, reports a slightly different version of Babylon's fall, saying that on the night Daniel interpreted the writing on the wall, Belshazzar was killed and a mysterious figure called Darius the Mede took over the kingdom. It is likely that Darius was, in fact, an alternative name for Cyrus.

The return of the exiles

The history of Judah itself during the period of Babylonian exile is poorly documented in the Bible. For a time the area seems to have been incorporated into the province of Samaria and there was intermittent war and infighting. Some people

Cyrus the Great built up his vast empire on a combination of military might and religious tolerance. His simple, austere tomb stands at Pasargadae near Persepolis, the capital of his successor, Darius the Great.

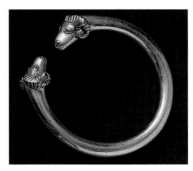

This solid gold bracelet with ends shaped like rams' heads was made by the Scythians who lived near the Caspian Sea. Precious objects such as this would have been paid to the Persian emperor as tribute.

The Persian Empire
The empire created when Cyrus captured territory from the Medes in the middle of the 6th century BCE, and extended by him and his successors, would not be surpassed until the time of Alexander the Great. To keep it together, excellent routes of communication were essential.

Greek sources speak of a 'Royal Road' from Susa to Sardis in Asia Minor. The Bible's account of the return of the first wave of Jews back to their homeland after their exile in Babylon is unclear, but the map below shows the routes they are most likely to have taken.

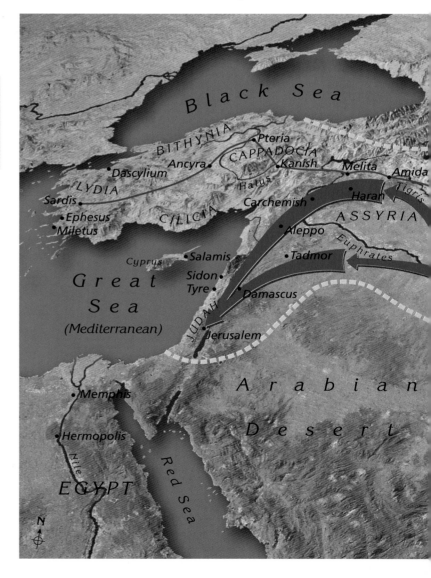

At Persepolis Darius the Great built a new palace and capital for the Persian empire. The most magnificent building was the Apadana, or audience hall (above left), where the kings of

subject peoples came every spring to present their tribute. The walls were decorated with formal friezes in relief, such as this (above right) depicting a lion attacking a bull.

The walls of Persepolis are richly ornamented with friezes in low relief illustrating the splendor and power of the Persian emperors. The 'Parade of the Nations' in the Apadana, Darius' principal audience hall, shows delegations from 23 subject nations bringing gifts ranging from clothing, metal vessels, gold, and elephant tusks to exotic animals such as okapi and antelope. The figure shown here may be a representative from the fabulously wealthy Lydians of western Asia Minor.

turned to other gods while others regarded the destruction of Jerusalem, and the exile of the Jewish elite, as God's judgment on their sins. On the whole, it was a dispirited community that greeted the exiles, and some even resented their return. It is not known how many Jews actually came back at this time, as many were well settled and prosperous in Babylon and chose to remain there, giving financial assistance to those who returned to their homeland.

The leader of the returning Jews, Sheshbazzar, was succeeded by Zerubbabel, and different sources credit each with laying the foundations of a new Temple − a development which delighted the people. But this elation was tempered by severe hardships. There was constant conflict with hostile neighbors and the harvests were poor. Little progress was made on rebuilding the city of Jerusalem or its walls until the time of Nehemiah and Ezra almost 100 years later.

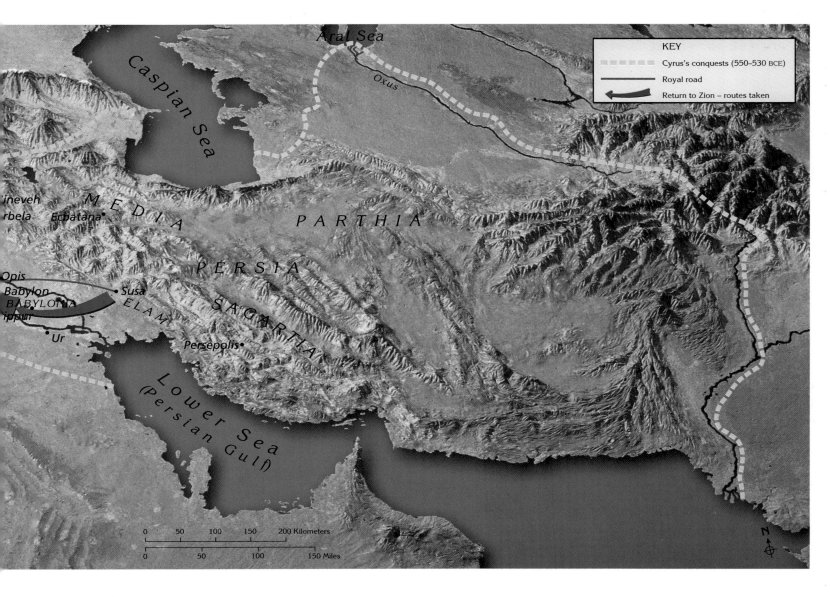

KEY

- - - - Cyrus's conquests (550–530 BCE)

———— Royal road

← Return to Zion – routes taken

Aral Sea

Oxus

Caspian Sea

ineveh
rbela   Ecbatana

MEDIA

PARTHIA

Opis
Babylon   Susa
BABYLONIA
ippun   ELAM

PERSIA

SAGARTIA

Ur

Persepolis

Lower Sea
(Persian Gulf)

0   50   100   150   200 Kilometers

0   50   100   150 Miles

N

Cupbearers at the court of the Persian king

The conquering of Babylon by Cyrus the Great in 539 BCE meant that Judah now fell under Persian control, eventually becoming the Persian province of Yehud. Cyrus sent many Jews exiled in Babylon back to Judah, and this policy was continued in the next century by a second wave of returning exiles under Artaxerxes, one of Cyrus' successors. It was this wave that would lead to the true refounding of the Jewish nation under the leadership of Nehemiah and Ezra.

Nehemiah, an exiled Jew, was a cupbearer at the court of Artaxerxes and had the ear of the king. When Nehemiah expressed concern for his homeland, particularly Jerusalem, which remained largely in ruins after its sack by Babylon, Artaxerxes decided to appoint him governor of Yehud with instructions to rebuild the city. This was in 445 BCE and Nehemiah returned to Jerusalem with many Jewish exiles taken from their settlements around Nippur in Babylonia. Under Nehemiah's enthusiastic governorship, Jerusalem's fortunes improved and the city walls were soon rebuilt.

Ezra was a priest rather than a political leader but in 457 BCE he, like Nehemiah, had also led some of the Jewish exiles home under Artaxerxes' instructions. If Nehemiah was responsible for the rebuilding of Jerusalem then to Ezra fell

■ I will save my people from the east country ... I will bring them to live in Jerusalem.

Zechariah 8:7–8

the task of reviving Judaism. Shocked by the lax religious practices of those who had remained in Judah, he instituted religious reforms based on the practices of the returning exiles, who had retained a strict religious code. The exiles were also horrified by the decline of Judaism in neighboring Samaria, where many Jews had adopted pagan ways.

Results of Ezra's reforms

Ezra's reforms ensured the survival of Judaism; indeed, he has been called the 'Father of Judaism' or a 'Second Moses' because the development of rabbinic Judaism is often traced back to his work. His reforms spread to several Jewish communities abroad, notably to Elephantine in Egypt. This colony was established in the 6th century BCE by Jews who had fled to escape the Babylonian invasion. In the intervening years they had adopted the worship of two goddesses as well as God, but they now turned to Ezra's more rigorous faith. In Babylon, the remaining Jewish community continued for many centuries as a center of Jewish life and learning.

The Cyrus Cylinder *from Babylon dates from 536 BCE. Made of clay, it records, in cuneiform script, the capture of the city by Cyrus the Great in 539 BCE. It also details his decree that the idols of gods* taken from cities throughout the empire should be returned, along with the exiled people who worshiped them. It was this decree that led to the repatriation of Jews from exile in Babylon around 538 BCE.

The Return to Jerusalem
Jews from the principal exile community in Nippur, near Babylon, returned to their homeland in two main waves: first under Sheshbazzar and Zerubbabel in 538–515 BCE, then under Nehemiah and Ezra in 457–428 BCE. The Judah to which they returned had become the Persian province of Yehud, part of the satrapy (administrative area) known as 'Beyond the River' – that is, the Euphrates. Even after this repatriation, large Jewish colonies remained in Babylon and at Elephantine in Egypt.

Elephantine Island *(below) at the First Cataract of the Nile in Egypt. Documents found here show that a community of Jews was living on the island after the conquest of Judah by the Babylonians in 586 BCE. The exile community adopted some Egyptian religious practices over the years, but returned to the true Jewish faith after news reached them of Ezra's religious reforms in Jerusalem.*

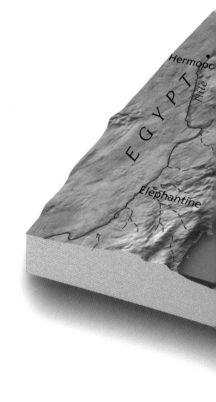

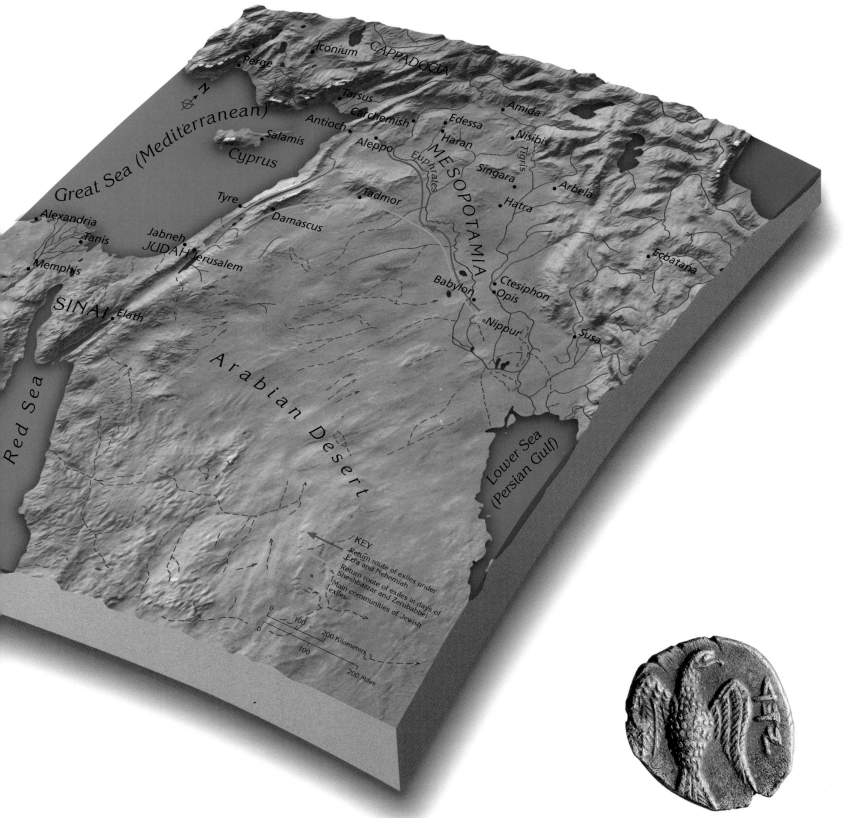

Great Sea (Mediterranean)

CAPPADOCIA

Perge
Iconium
Tarsus
Antioch
Carchemish
Salamis
Cyprus
Aleppo
Edessa
Haran
Amida
Nisibis
Tigris
Singara
MESOPOTAMIA
Euphrates
Arbela
Tadmor
Hatra
Tyre
Damascus
Alexandria
Tanis
Jabneh
JUDAH
Jerusalem
Memphis
SINAI
Elath
Babylon
Ctesiphon
Opis
Nippur
Ecbatana
Susa

Red Sea

Arabian Desert

Lower Sea
(Persian Gulf)

KEY
Return route of exiles under
Ezra and Nehemiah
Return route of exiles in days of
Sheshbazzar and Zerubbabel
Main communities of Jewish
exiles

0   100   200 Kilometers
0   100   200 Miles

Remains of Ahab's palace in the city of Samaria. The returning Jewish exiles found that their neighbors in Samaria had intermarried with pagan peoples and had rejected Judaism in favor of pagan religious practices.

A Persian coin from Yehud decorated with an eagle on one side and a lily on the other. Coins such as this were issued in Jerusalem for use in the new Persian province of Yehud, created from the former Jewish kingdom of Judah.

A coin with the head of Alexander

In 334 BCE Alexander, son of Philip II of Macedon, crossed from Europe into Anatolia with about 30,000 foot soldiers and 5000 cavalry. His aim was the destruction of the Persian empire. After victories over the Persian governors of Asia Minor at the River Grancus, and then over the Persian emperor Darius III at Issus, Alexander advanced south toward Egypt destroying Phoenician cities in his path. Only Tyre, which fell after a 17-month siege, offered any resistance.

Alexander continued his march through Persian controlled Galilee, Samaria, and Ashdod (the former Philistia). The city of Gaza held out for two months, and once it fell he massacred its citizens in retaliation. Finally Alexander reached Egypt, which submitted without resistance. Alexander was proclaimed the new Pharaoh and he spent the winter of 332–331 BCE in Egypt, during which time he founded the city

of Alexandria. He then left once again for Tyre. On the way, he is said to have visited Jerusalem, and he is known to have crushed mercilessly a rebellion in Samaria. The city of Samaria itself was sacked and its citizens killed or enslaved.

In 331 BCE he crossed the River Euphrates and headed for the Persian heartland. He defeated Darius again at Gaugamela, after which the Persian emperor was assassinated by his own sons. Alexander then formally declared himself emperor of Persia. He continued his campaign by marching east across

*The **Alexander Mosaic**, found in Pompeii and thought to be a copy of a 4th-century BCE Greek painting, depicts Alexander's victory over the Persian king Darius III in battle.*

In the detail, below left, Alexander leads the decisive charge of the Macedonian cavalry, while, below right, Darius is shown preparing to turn his chariot in flight.

The Conquests of Alexander
The great empire created by Alexander was the largest the world had yet seen. His army of Macedonian and Greek troops overthrew the far-flung but disunited Persian empire within a period of four years. This campaign took him from Asia Minor to Egypt and then eastward to Central Asia and the Indus valley of India. Wherever he went, Alexander founded or refounded Greek-style cities with his own name, spreading Hellenistic city-based culture over the whole empire.

the Hindu Kush mountains into the Indus valley in northern India in 326 BCE. Here his troops mutinied so Alexander led his remnant army across the southern Persian desert back to Babylon, where he died suddenly in 323 BCE at the age of 32.

Alexander's successors in Palestine
Alexander's death was followed by continual fighting among rival claimants to his empire for the next four decades. In Macedonia, Antigonus One-Eye tried to reunite the empire, while the Greek general Ptolemy – the son of Alexander's governor in Egypt – sought a separate empire for himself. Between 315 and 306 BCE the armies of these two protagonists campaigned back and forth in Palestine and Syria. By the early 3rd century BCE Ptolemy had secured his hold on Egypt and had brought Palestine under his control, administering it and Syria from Alexandria. These areas were also claimed by Seleucus, another of Alexander's rival generals, who now ruled the eastern part of the former empire.

Throughout all this upheaval, Judah continued as a theocracy, with authority vested in the High Priest and with priests having civil as well as religious responsibilities. This was a creative, literary period in Judah, with the Book of Ecclesiastes and the first Jewish Apocalypse – an account of the end of the world – dating from this time. The translation of the Hebrew scriptures into Greek, the Septuagint, is said

to have been initiated by Ptolemy II during this period, but was probably carried out in Egypt rather than Palestine.

Early in the 2nd century BCE the Ptolemies finally lost Palestine to the Seleucids under Antiochus III (223–187 BCE). The Jews initially supported Antiochus and received legal and religious favors in return. By the 170s BCE, however, Seleucid pressure on the Jews to adopt Greek culture was leading to unrest between Hellenized and conservative Jews, and a general Jewish resentment of their Seleucid masters.

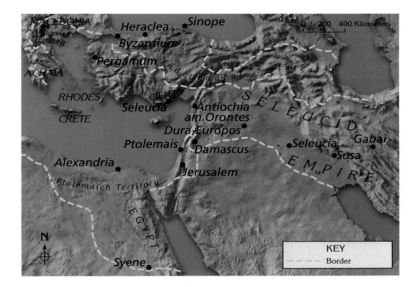

The Seleucid Empire
The Seleucid empire (above) eventually became the largest of the successor empires after the death of Alexander. Syria and Palestine had initially been ruled by the Ptolemies of Egypt, but were conquered by the Seleucid Antiochus III in 201–198 BCE. They remained under Seleucid rule for the next 31 years. In the meantime, the Seleucids extended their rule into Asia Minor and Greece, only to be expelled by the new rising power, Rome.

A Macedonian cavalryman in action in a detail from the 'Alexander Sarcophagus.' Found in Sidon, and now in the Archeological Museum in Istanbul, this finely carved sarcophagus is thought to be that of an unknown Macedonian nobleman.

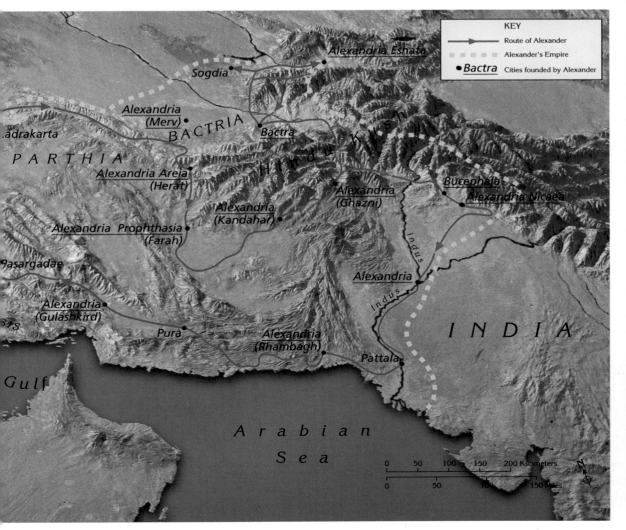

Torah scroll of the 19th century from Iraq

Judaism first encountered Greek culture, or 'Hellenism,' through the Diaspora, the dispersion of the Jewish people as a result of events in their turbulent history. The centuries between the exile of the Jews in Babylon in 597 BCE and the time of Herod the Great in the first century BCE, saw this dispersion of Jews to many parts of the ancient world. By the end of this period, about half the estimated total of seven million Jews lived outside Palestine, notably in Babylon and Alexandria. Over the years, these exiles embraced many elements of Hellenistic civilization, particularly the Greek language which was the language of learning and also widely used in commerce.

Hellenism in Palestine

When Alexander the Great's army conquered Judea around 332 BCE, the influence of Hellenism on the Jews increased. To be successful in the world that Alexander had created, one needed a Greek education. Many Jews accepted this happily enough – Philo of Alexandria (*c.*20 BCE–50 CE), for example, combined Jewish beliefs with Greek philosophical ideas. Jewish High Priests were also pleased to welcome Hellenized Jews to the Temple when they returned on pilgrimage. But more conservative Jews deplored Greek customs such as athletics and wrestling, regarding Hellenism as a threat to their way of life. Partly as a result of this ferment, a variety of new religious groups emerged within Judaism, the most influential of these being the Pharisees and the Sadducees.

■ The Sadducees say that there is no resurrection, or angel, or spirit; but the Pharisees acknowledge all three.

Acts 23:8

Pharisees and Sadducees

The Pharisees reacted against Hellenistic influence by insisting on the strict observance of Jewish ritual laws. They punctiliously obeyed rules on food and purity, and many kept themselves apart from non-Pharisees as a result. Despite this, the Pharisees enjoyed popular support among the people and were influential in the Jews' supreme court and legislative body, the Sanhedrin.

The Pharisees laid the foundations of rabbinic Judaism, using the synagogue as a center for religious teaching. They placed emphasis on the traditional oral interpretation of the scriptures, called the 'Oral Torah,' believing it to have been handed down from the time of Moses. The Pharisees also popularized a new perception of God as being concerned with the individual and not just the nation.

The Greek pottery vessels *above are decorated with images of men drinking (left) and a wrestling scene (right). The pervasive influence of Hellenistic culture meant that some Jews adopted Greek customs. Although Jewish youths participated in Greek activities such as wrestling, conservative Jews disapproved of their taking part, objecting that they indicated a decadent lifestyle. Greek wrestling, for example, was conducted in the nude. Such practices were regarded as a threat to the Jewish religion and way of life, and were actively discouraged.*

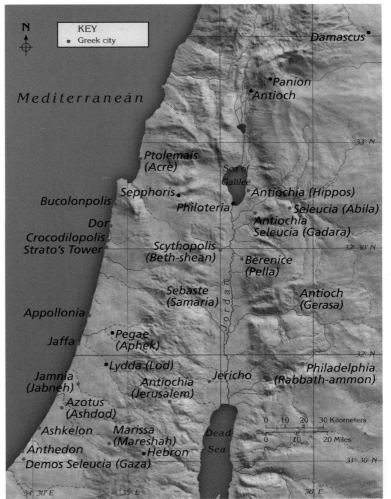

This Roman mosaic from the synagogue at Beth-shean depicts two important symbols of Judaism: the menorah and the Temple. Despite the influence of Hellenism both at home in Palestine and in the lands of the Diaspora, the Jewish people generally remained true to their faith.

Hellenistic Palestine
From the time of Alexander the Great, the Jewish world came increasingly under the influence of Greek culture and learning. Many Jews became Hellenized, speaking Greek and adopting Greek customs. This map shows the impact of Greek influence on Palestine. Hellenistic culture spread across the region through the establishment of new cities with Greek names such as Scythopolis and Ptolemais. Hellenistic cities are shown on the map by red dots.

The Sadducees are thought to have derived their name from Zadok, High Priest during Solomon's time. Although there were only a few thousand Sadducees, they exercised considerable political and spiritual influence, being mainly from wealthy backgrounds and including among their number the High Priest, in effect the president of the Sanhedrin. Unlike the Pharisees, the Sadducees accepted only the authority of the 'Written Torah,' that is the first five books of the Bible and selected other writings on Jewish wisdom. Also, in contrast to the Pharisees, the Sadducees rejected the idea of resurrection, angels, and spirits.

Opposition to Hellenism in Palestine resulted in the strengthening of Judaism by the emergence of such groups that promoted the religion. But Hellenistic rule also led to the voluntary dispersion of the Jews. The network of trade routes across the Greek empire encouraged merchant Jews to leave Palestine. Emigrants took their religion with them, thereby helping to spread Judaism throughout the known world, resulting in the conversion of a number of Gentiles.

The Torah
The word Torah means 'teaching' and originally referred only to the first five books of the Old Testament – the 'Pentateuch.' The Pharisees, a strict religious group within Judaism, followed the teaching of the Oral Torah, namely the traditional interpretation of scriptures handed down from generation to generation since the time of Moses. They applied the Torah to everyday contemporary life by constant reinterpretation. This was one of the reasons they were opposed by the Sadducees who, by contrast, placed primary emphasis on the written word, following the letter of the law in the Written Torah. Later, the Torah came to

include the books of wisdom and works of rabbinic learning. Collectively, this is what makes up the modern Torah today. But the Torah has always been more than a set of laws: it lays down a way of life based on the covenant God made with his people. An ancient Torah manuscript is shown above.

Antiochus Epiphanes IV portrayed on a coin

In 323 BCE, Alexander the Great died and his generals divided his empire between themselves. In the Middle East, Ptolemy founded a ruling dynasty in Egypt, Syria, and Phoenicia, while Seleucus ruled in Mesopotamia. At first, Judea was part of the dominion of Ptolemy and his successors, but by 200 BCE the Seleucid king Antiochus III had taken over the area. Under Seleucid rule pressure on the Jews to adopt Hellenistic culture increased.

When Antiochus IV acceded in 175 BCE, he launched an attack on the Jewish religion, perhaps out of greed for the wealth of its Temple in Jerusalem, or perhaps out of extreme megalomania. He also claimed divine status and took the title

At the battle of Elasa, 161 BCE, the Maccabean army was defeated by superior Seleucid forces and Judas Maccabeus was killed. His brothers Jonathan and Simon placed his body in the tomb of their ancestors, which, according to tradition, is this stone tomb at Modein near Lod.

Maccabean Campaigns
The map below shows the most significant areas involved in the Maccabean campaigns against the Seleucid dynasty. In about 167 BCE, the Jews rose in revolt against their Seleucid rulers led by the family of Mattathias. The rebels became known as the Maccabeans. The struggle would continue for 25 years until Seleucid infighting led to their loss of Judea.

■ 'Judas Maccabeus has been a mighty warrior from his youth; he shall command the army for you and fight the battle against the peoples.'

1 Maccabees 2:66

of Epiphanes meaning 'God manifest.' His enemies, however, preferred to call him Epimanes – 'the Mad one.'

In 169 BCE, Antiochus plundered the Temple, and the following year trouble flared up in Jerusalem. Antiochus sent in troops who looted the city and pulled down its walls. The invaders used the Temple to worship the Greek god Zeus, and pagan altars were set up across the country. Jews were compelled to worship idols and to take part in pagan sacrifices. Jewish sacrifices and observance of the Sabbath were forbidden.

Rebellion at Modein
Jews who resisted these edicts were persecuted and eventually rebellion flared, starting in the village of Modein. Here lived the priestly Mattathias and his five sons, John, Simon, Judas, Eleazar, and Jonathan. When officials came to enforce Antiochus' pagan sacrifices, Mattathias refused to take part. He killed a Seleucid official and a Jew who followed Antiochus' orders, then destroyed the pagan altar. Calling on all true Jews to join him he fled into the hills with his sons. From here Mattathias began to wage a guerilla war against both the Seleucids and collaborating Jews.

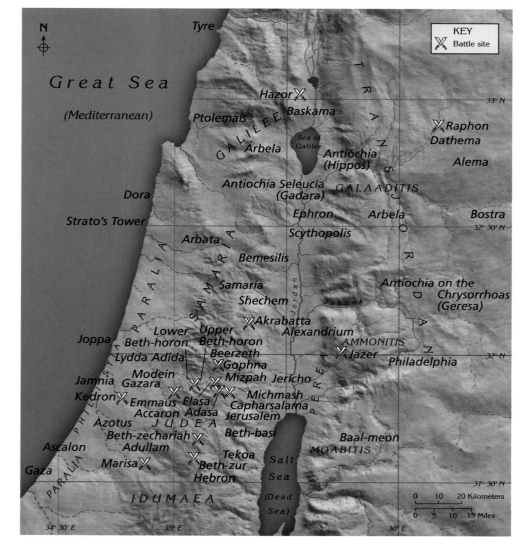

Matthathias died in 166 BCE but his third son, Judas, known as Maccabeus – 'the Hammer' – took command of the resistance forces and attacked the Seleucid army vigorously. He marched on Jerusalem and won back the Temple, which his followers, now known as the Maccabeans, then repurified. This act is still celebrated in the feast of Chanukah.

Then, in 163 BCE, Maccabean fortunes turned and Judas was defeated by Seleucid forces at Beth-zechariah. His brother Eleazar was killed and Judas was forced to flee. The Seleucids re-established some control in Jerusalem and, although hampered by divisive power struggles among their leaders, won a major victory at the battle of Elasa in 161 BCE, where Judas Maccabeus himself was killed.

Despite this blow, Jonathan and Simon, the last two of Judas's brothers, continued the fight. Over the following years they were helped by increasing internal dissensions in the Seleucid camp. This significantly weakened Seleucid power, forcing them to make ever greater concessions to the Maccabeans. Eventually, in 142 BCE, finding their position untenable, the Seleucids granted independence to Judea.

The Maccabean rebellion was sparked off when officials came to Modein to ensure that pagan sacrifices ordered by Antiochus IV were carried out. In this illustration from a manuscript of the Book of Maccabees, *made in the 10th century by monks of St Gallen, Switzerland, Mattathias raises his sword to kill the villager who came forward to sacrifice what appears to be a pig – an animal regarded as unclean by the Jews – at the pagan altar. At the top of the picture, Mattathias kills one of the king's officials.*

This fragment of a Greek vase painting depicts a pagan ceremony in which a procession is leading a sacrificial bull to the altar. The monotheistic Jews were exposed to the pagan religion of the cultures that surrounded them from as early as the time of Abraham. During the 2nd century BCE, the Seleucid leader, Antiochus IV, attempted to unify his empire by spreading Greek civilization. Jews were forced to take part in pagan ceremonies and were prohibited from practicing their own faith. The Jewish people's refusal to follow Antiochus IV's edicts resulted in rebellion.

At Beth-zechariah the Seleucid army used Indian war elephants – like the one in this 3rd-century BCE terracotta statuette from Myrina, western Asia Minor – against the Maccabean forces. During the battle, Judas' brother Eleazar saw what he mistakenly thought was the Seleucid king's own elephant. He managed to get beneath it and stab it in the belly but was crushed to death when the dying elephant collapsed on top of him.

Jean Hyrcanus became king of Judea in 104 BCE succeeding his father, Simon Maccabee. Judea was now independent from Syria, and John and his successors, also called the Hasmoneans, pursued a policy of territorial expansion and the forcible conversion to Judaism of their conquered subjects. As time went on, the Hasmoneans split into factions, warring both with themselves and their neighbors.

Detail of carving found at Herod's palace, Herodium

In 63 BCE, the Roman general Pompey intervened. He took Jerusalem, the Judean capital, in a brutal siege and installed his own ruler, a government official called Antipater, the son of an enforced convert to Judaism. Although Judea was now a client state of Rome, Pompey did allow it to preserve a certain amount of its traditional government by priests.

Antipater's son, Herod, was given charge of the northern region of Galilee. Then, after Antipater's death, Rome recognized Herod as king of all Judea. Herod imposed this foreign decision on the country by capturing Jerusalem, with Roman help, in 37 BCE. His position, however, was not completely secure. In the wars that followed the assassination of Julius Caesar, Herod sided with Mark Antony against Octavian, Caesar's nephew and official heir. After Antony's defeat, Herod had to ask pardon from Octavian, later Rome's first emperor, Augustus, before his kingship was confirmed.

Herod, known as 'the Great' because he was the eldest son, could be ruthless, but he was a good administrator,

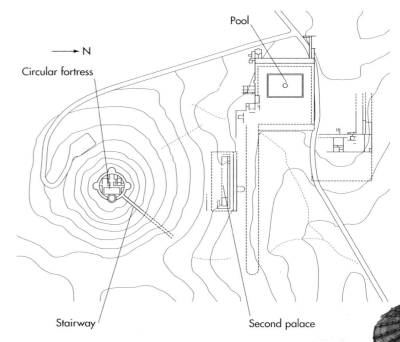

Pool
N
Circular fortress
Stairway
Second palace

Semicircular tower

The groundplan *(above) shows Herod's circular fortress in relation to Lower Herodium, at the foot of the hill on the north side. This area contained various buildings including a second palace and a large pool which was used both for bathing and as a reservoir.*

Herod's Fortress
This reconstruction of Herod's fortress at Herodium is based on archeological remains. It was constructed on an artificial mound on the summit of an existing hill. The fortress was intended for use as a bolt-hole if Herod's life were ever threatened, and was also destined to be his mausoleum. Herod's body was brought here, as Josephus the historian describes, but his tomb has never been found.

Herod's Kingdom
At his death in 4 BCE, Herod the Great's kingdom had reached its maximum extent. It included Judea, Samaria and Galilee, and stretched from the boundary of Syria in the north to the kingdom of Nabatea in the south. The map shows Herod's territory at this point and the location of Herodium and other fortresses that he built. Lying to the southeast of Bethlehem, Herodium was one of the most impressive of Herod's many constructions.

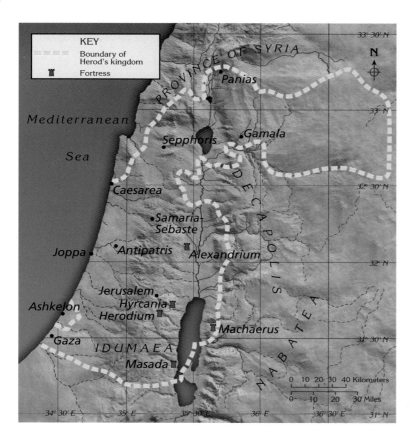

KEY
Boundary of Herod's kingdom
Fortress

PROVINCE OF SYRIA
Panias
Mediterranean
Sepphoris
Gamala
Sea
DECAPOLIS
Caesarea
Samaria Sebaste
Joppa
Antipatris
Alexandrium
Jerusalem
Hyrcania
Ashkelon
Herodium
Machaerus
Gaza
IDUMAEA
Masada
NABATEA

0 10 20 30 40 Kilometers
0 10 20 30 Miles

Artificial mound

skillfully balancing the demands of the various groups on whom he depended for power. He aimed to make his mark with the construction of great buildings – most notably the Temple in Jerusalem – but also with defensive works such as the fortress at Herodium to the southeast of Bethlehem. But Herod's monuments did not last long. He died in 4 BCE, and just over 70 years later the Temple which he had built, and many of his other buildings, were destroyed by the Romans when they ruthlessly crushed the Jewish revolt.

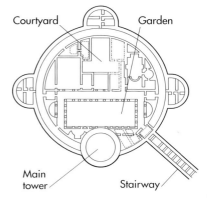

Courtyard   Garden

Main tower   Stairway

The plan of Herodium (left) shows the layout of the fortress. The interior was divided into two sections. In the area beneath the main round tower there was a garden surrounded by columns. The other half of the palace was divided by a cross-shaped courtyard. The only access to the fortress was via an underground stairway rising from the base of the hill.

The well-preserved remains of Herodium as seen from the air. The cone-shaped hill, which resembles a volcano, rises some 758m (2500 ft) above sea level and is a distinctive landmark.

Main tower

Cross-shaped courtyard

Bathhouse

Storerooms

Garden

Stairway entrance

Byzantine mosaic showing the resurrected Jesus Christ

The New Testament consists of 27 books most of which were probably written between 50 and 100 CE. It opens with the four Gospels, accounts of the life and teachings of Jesus Christ. The Acts of the Apostles follows, continuing the story after Jesus' death and resurrection, describing how Jesus' early followers began to spread his message and establish Christian communities, or churches, throughout the Graeco-Roman world. The rest of the New Testament consists of letters offering advice and encouragement to these new churches from various writers, predominantly Paul of Tarsus. It ends with the Book of Revelation, a visionary account of the Day of Judgment and the coming of God's kingdom.

The Gospels

The main details of Jesus' life are told in the Gospels, ascribed to the evangelists Matthew, Mark, Luke, and John. The Gospels are not systematic biographies of Jesus, but were intended to instill and defend the Christian faith. To suit this purpose the Gospel writers selected various significant incidents from Jesus' life to show that he was the Son of God and the Christ, or Messiah. Contemporary Jews expected such a savior to deliver them from their enemies and then to usher in a new world order. Even though the Gospels offer only a scant retelling of Jesus' life, the reader can still form an idea of both the man and his times from the often evocative accounts of Jesus' preaching and conversations, his traveling, his friends and details about everyday life.

How and by whom the Gospels were written

The Gospel stories ultimately derive from oral accounts of Jesus' acts and teaching that were preserved by his closest

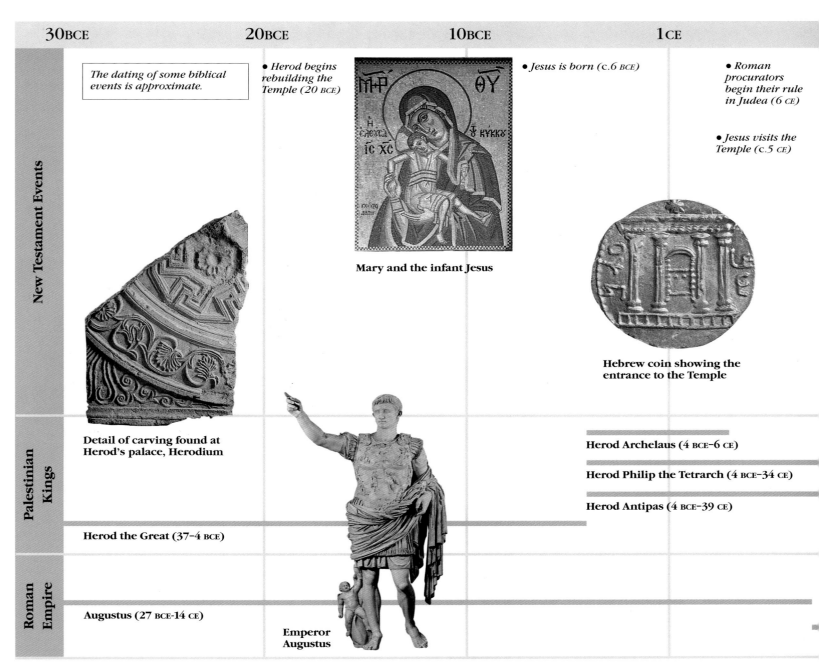

30BCE	20BCE	10BCE	1CE

New Testament Events

The dating of some biblical events is approximate.

● *Herod begins rebuilding the Temple (20 BCE)*

● *Jesus is born (c.6 BCE)*

● *Roman procurators begin their rule in Judea (6 CE)*

● *Jesus visits the Temple (c.5 CE)*

Mary and the infant Jesus

Hebrew coin showing the entrance to the Temple

Detail of carving found at Herod's palace, Herodium

Palestinian Kings

Herod Archelaus (4 BCE–6 CE)

Herod Philip the Tetrarch (4 BCE–34 CE)

Herod Antipas (4 BCE–39 CE)

Herod the Great (37–4 BCE)

Roman Empire

Augustus (27 BCE–14 CE)

Emperor Augustus

followers. Initially, important incidents would have been memorized and transmitted by word of mouth. Eventually these oral accounts were written down, probably in Greek.

Scholars debate which Gospel was written first. Most agree that Mark was the earliest and was then used by the writers of Matthew and Luke for their own versions, along with another source, now lost, known simply as 'Q.' Because of their similarities, these three accounts are referred to as the Synoptic Gospels (from the Greek meaning 'seeing together'). The fourth Gospel, John, differs in style and content from the Synoptics. It includes incidents the others do not, such as Jesus turning water into wine at Cana. It is also more theological, examining in detail Jesus' relationship with God.

The identities of the Gospel writers are not certain. The Gospels are all anonymous and names were attributed to them some time after they were written. The names Matthew and John may refer to apostles, Mark is thought to have been Peter's interpreter, while Luke was an associate of Paul.

Acts of the Apostles and the letters

The Acts of the Apostles, also attributed to Luke, describes how the Christian faith was spread, principally by Paul and his companions. Acts is followed by 21 letters, or epistles, written to the early churches to encourage them in their faith. Paul is accredited with 13 of these epistles (although scholars doubt whether he was the author of all of them), which include some of the most impassioned and personal writing in the Bible. Of the remaining letters, seven are ascribed to other important Christian figures and one is anonymous.

The New Testament ends with The Book of Revelation, an inspiring, mysterious text, full of symbolism and strange images, about God's plan for humanity's eventual salvation.

By the 2nd century CE many Christian texts, including the Gospels, were in circulation. The early church fathers debated the validity of these texts, rejecting some and including others, until by about the 4th century CE they had established the New Testament structure as we know it today.

20CE	40CE	60CE	80CE	100CE

● *Jesus begins his ministry* (c.28)

● *John the Baptist executed* (c.28)

● *Jesus is crucified* (c.30)

● *Paul converted to Christianity* (c.34)

Gospel of Mark written (c.60–c.70)

Gospels of Matthew and Luke and Acts of the Apostles written (c.70–c.80)

John's Gospel and Book of Revelation written (c.90–c.100)

Roman carving of a transport ship, typical of Paul's day

Paul's first missionary journey (46–48)

Paul's second missionary journey (50–52)

First Jewish Revolt (66–70)

Paul's third missionary journey (53–57)

● *Temple at Jerusalem destroyed (70)*

Paul imprisoned in Rome (59–c.61)

Paul's letters (50–60)

● *Paul dies (c.65)*

Christ's crucifixion

Herod Agrippa I (37–44)

Roman soldiers with relics from the sack of Jerusalem

Herod Agrippa II (50–100)

Pontius Pilate procurator of Judea (26–36)

Claudius (41–54)

Galba (68–69) Otho (69) Vitellius (69)

Titus (79–81)

Caligula (37–41)

Tiberius (14–37)

Nero (54–68)

Vespasian (69–79)

Domitian (81–96)

Coin portraying Emperor Augustus

The world into which Jesus was born was dominated by Rome, the capital of the most powerful empire in the Western world. From the Atlantic coast of Spain in the west to the Black Sea in the east, from the Rhine in the north to the Nile in the south, the Romans controlled vast swathes of land in which the towns were linked by a highly developed network of well-constructed roads. At its heart, the Mediterranean Sea was practically a Roman lake, entirely surrounded by imperial territory.

By the time of the death of Augustus, the first Roman emperor, in 14 CE, the Empire had almost reached its greatest extent. It consisted of 36 provinces governed by officials responsible either to the Senate, the Empire's legislative council, or to the emperor himself. These governors ruled with the aid of an efficient bureaucracy and a powerful, well-equipped army that kept public order as well as helping to collect taxes. The *Pax Romana*, or 'Roman Peace,' which had

Augustus
Portraits and statues of the Emperor Augustus produced during his lifetime show him as a paternalistic yet youthful figure. He is depicted as no older than 33, the age at which he became the first Roman emperor. Augustus (the name means 'Revered one') came to be regarded as semidivine, an idea that was encouraged by later emperors in order to increase their own authority.

been established by Augustus, enabled trade to flourish across the Empire – trade that was assisted by monetary control and well-maintained roads and ports.

Rome's empire was essentially an urban one, and Roman cities throughout the territory shared common features. There was the forum, originally the central market place, which served as the town's social and political center; there

were baths, with hot and cold rooms; an amphitheater, where gladiatorial and other displays were mounted; and perhaps a library and basilica, or public hall. The Romans were accomplished architects and engineers, using bricks, stone, and concrete to build magnificent temples, bridges, roads, aqueducts, drainage systems, and other civic structures.

In the east, the Romans brought peace and prosperity. The one exception in this region was Judea, which became a Roman province in 6 CE. Loyal to their God and to their Law, the Jews found the yoke of pagan Roman rule hard to bear, even though Judaism was given special status under Roman law. Jews were exempt from military service, for instance, and were excused court appearances on the Sabbath. Despite these measures, Jewish nationalism remained strong and anti-Roman feeling was exacerbated by a series of corrupt and insensitive governors, of whom Pontius Pilate was one. Unrest finally flared up into the great rebellion of 66 CE. This uprising was mercilessly crushed by the Romans in a violent response that culminated in 70 CE with the complete destruction of Jerusalem and its magnificent Temple.

The Roman Empire
In 14 CE, when Augustus died, the Roman Empire comprised some 36 provinces (left). One of Augustus' aims was to create effective government for Rome and its provinces alike, and he himself appointed the officials who governed the eastern provinces such as Judea (right) and Syria.

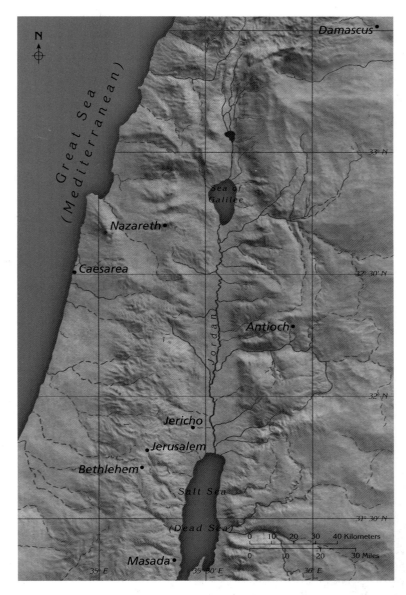

Roman cities *in the eastern provinces shared many of the standard features of provincial cities throughout the empire. This colonnaded and well-paved avenue at Palmyra in Syria (right) and the triumphal arch in the centre of Volubilis in Morocco (below), provide excellent examples of Roman architectural and engineering skills as well as civic pride.*

The amphitheater, *venue for gladiatorial combat and other cruel and bloody sports, played a vital part in Roman social life. These ruins at El-Jem Tunisia (right) still reveal a fine example of a typical provincial city amphitheater.*

The Virgin Mary and the infant Jesus

The story of Jesus' birth in the town of Bethlehem in Judea is one of the most cherished of Christian traditions, forming the basis of annual Christmas celebrations throughout the world. But, despite its familiarity, much uncertainty hangs over the event. Only the Gospels of Matthew and Luke describe Jesus' birth; those of Mark and John make no mention of it at all.

Luke describes how Mary, a young woman from Nazareth, was chosen to be the mother of Jesus. An angel appeared to her and said she would bear a child through the Holy Spirit. Matthew says that an angel appeared to Joseph, Mary's

■ The angel said to her, 'Do not be afraid, Mary ... And now, you will conceive in your womb and bear a son, and you will name him Jesus. He will be great, and will be called the Son of the Most High.'

Luke 1:30

betrothed, telling him not to reject her; she had not been unfaithful – her child had been conceived by the Holy Spirit. They were instructed to call the baby Jesus.

The Nativity

Luke says that Jesus was born during the reign of Emperor Augustus (30 BCE–14 CE). As part of a census Joseph and Mary went to Joseph's ancestral town of Bethlehem to register. The town was so crowded when they arrived that they could not find any accommodation and had to lodge in a stable. Mary had her baby there and laid the child in a manger, an animal feeding box. The first witnesses to Jesus' birth were local shepherds, instructed by an angel to visit the holy child.

The Magi present their gifts to the infant Jesus, in a mosaic from Ravenna in Italy. The Bible does not say how many Magi there were, but later tradition says there were three, and calls them kings. The 'Magi' were originally a tribe within the Persian empire, famed for their skill in astrology.

Matthew focuses on the Magi, or wise men, who journeyed from the East. They followed a star which they interpreted as heralding the birth of a king of the Jews. When Herod the Great (37–4 BCE), the Jewish ruler of Palestine, heard of the Magi and their quest he was disturbed by the possibility of a rival to his throne. Informed that the prophet Micah had predicted that the new 'ruler' would be born in

Star of Bethlehem
The nature of the star that guided the Magi to the stable in Bethlehem where Jesus was born continues to stimulate debate. Some astronomers argue that the star could have been a comet. Although there are no independent reports of comets in the year of Jesus' birth, it has been calculated that Halley's Comet, shown left – the brightest regularly returning comet in the solar system – appeared in 12 BCE, about six years before Jesus is thought to have been born. The broken line in the diagram to the right shows the orbit of Halley's Comet in relation to the orbital planes of the planets Earth, Jupiter, and Neptune. It has also been suggested that the star could have been a supernova, a star that explodes with a sudden increase in brightness. Another theory is that the star was a conjunction between planets – that is, two planets appearing to move close together – a phenomenon that can appear as a single, radiant source of light. The early 17th-century German astronomer Johannes Kepler calculated that the planets Jupiter and Saturn were in conjunction in the year 7 BCE, and also that Venus and Jupiter were in conjunction in 3 BCE. None of these proposed natural phenomena satisfactorily explains the description of the star in Matthew's Gospel. But, regardless of its origins, the star is an important element in the accounts of the birth of Jesus. As the Magi recognized, it was a sign that something of great import was about to happen.

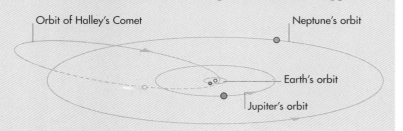

Orbit of Halley's Comet   Neptune's orbit

Earth's orbit

Jupiter's orbit

The small town of Bethlehem seen above as it is today, and above right in an old photograph. Some old buildings and streets appear very little changed from Jesus' day. Bethlehem lies 8km (5 miles) south of Jerusalem among the fertile hills and valleys of Judea. According to Luke's Gospel, it was in these hills that a shining angel appeared to a group of shepherds and told them of Jesus' birth.

Bethlehem, Herod summoned the Magi and told them to search for the child there. He then asked them to report back to him, saying that he wished to honor the child. The Magi duly found Mary and Jesus and presented them with gifts of gold, myrrh, and frankincense, representing Jesus' kingship, death, and resurrection. They then went home by a different route, having been warned in a dream not to return to Herod.

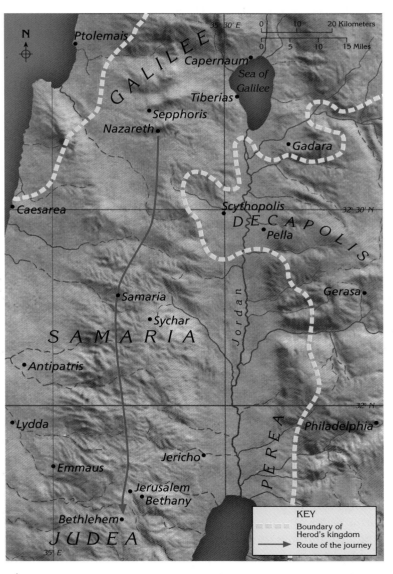

The Church of the Nativity in Bethlehem is said to stand over the place where Jesus was born. This church, built in the 6th century by the Emperor Justinian, occupies the site of an earlier church dedicated in 339 CE by Helena, mother of Constantine the Great, the first Christian emperor of Rome.

In the crypt of the Church of the Nativity, beneath the altar, lies a silver star set in marble. The star bears an inscription relating to the birth of Jesus. The church was plundered of much of its decoration after the Crusader period, but was restored toward the end of the 19th century.

The Journey to Bethlehem
According to the Gospel of Luke, around the time of Jesus' birth a census was conducted by Quirinius, the Roman governor of Syria. The census required people to register in their ancestral towns. Joseph, though resident in Nazareth in Galilee, belonged to the House of David, and his family roots lay in the town of Bethlehem in Judea. He was therefore obliged, along with Mary – at that time heavily pregnant – to make the long journey to Bethlehem about 120km (80 miles) to the south, through the region of Samaria.

Mosaic showing the flight of the holy family to Egypt

Only Matthew's and Luke's Gospels describe the events that followed Jesus' birth, but their accounts differ quite dramatically. Luke relates that the holy family went to the Temple in Jerusalem to carry out certain religious rituals, while Matthew says that, fearing for their safety, Joseph, Mary, and the new-born Jesus fled to Egypt under instructions from an angel.

Presentation at the Temple

According to Luke, Jesus was circumcised and given his name on the eighth day after he was born: 'Jesus' is the Greek equivalent of the Hebrew name Joshua, meaning 'the Lord saves.' The family then made the short journey from Bethlehem to Jerusalem to visit the Temple and to perform two rituals. The first concerned Mary, who was obliged to make a small sacrifice to mark the end of her period of 'impurity' following the birth of a child. In the second ceremony, known as the 'redemption of the first-born,' Jesus

■ Master, now you are dismissing your servant in peace, according to your word, for my eyes have seen your salvation ...
Luke 2:29–30

was 'presented' to God because Jewish Law stipulated that first-born males, human and animal, are holy to the Lord.

On arriving at the Temple courts, the family met an elderly man named Simeon, who had been told by the Holy Spirit that he would not die until he had seen the Messiah. When Simeon saw Jesus he immediately recognized him as the Christ who would bring salvation, took him in his arms, and praised God. Simeon then blessed the family, predicting that Jesus would have a turbulent life and cause his mother much suffering.

No sooner had Simeon left them than an 84-year-old widow named Anna approached the family. Anna was a prophetess, and she too recognized Jesus as the Christ and spoke about him to everyone who was seeking redemption. After this, and with their rituals duly completed, Joseph, Mary, and Jesus set off for their home town of Nazareth in Galilee.

The flight into Egypt

Matthew's account of the events after Jesus' birth is very different. He tells of Joseph being warned in a dream by an angel that Herod the Great intended to kill Jesus. Herod, appointed by Rome as king of Judea, had heard from the Magi that a new king had been born and feared that the child would eventually usurp him. He had therefore decreed that all boys under two should be killed. To avoid this terrible fate,

the holy family fled to Egypt. Matthew gives no details of the journey itself, nor of where the family stayed in Egypt, or what they did there, but as a result of their swift action they succeeded in escaping Herod's 'Massacre of the Innocents.' They remained in Egypt until an angel advised Joseph that Herod was dead and that it was now safe to return to Israel. Joseph and his family set out for Nazareth, taking care not to linger in Judea, where Herod's son and successor, Archelaus, was proving to be as cruel a despot as his father had been.

Jesus' upbringing

The Gospels say very little about Jesus' early life in Nazareth. This small town, nestling in a hollow among limestone hills and surrounded by fertile fields, was a typical rural Galilean settlement: a conglomeration of predominantly one-storey houses, divided by narrow streets, with a market place and a synagogue. Though somewhat sleepy and isolated, the town overlooked the main highway from Damascus to Egypt and the coast, and so would have received news from the world outside fairly quickly. Only 6 kilometers (4 miles) to the northwest was Sepphoris, where Herod Antipas, the ruler of Galilee, had his court until 22 CE.

Very little is known of the early life of Jesus, but he probably followed his father's trade of carpentry. As a Jew, he would have attended the local synagogue and learned the stories of the rich sacred history of Israel. Although there is no record of him having any formal rabbinic training, Jesus was renowned for his knowledge of the Jewish Law.

Luke does have one account of Jesus as a boy at 12 years old on the family's annual visit to Jerusalem for the Passover. His parents began their journey home not realizing Jesus had stayed behind in the Temple. Here they finally found him, discussing the Law with learned men, who were amazed by his understanding. Jesus chided his worried parents, saying they should have known he would be in his Father's house. This is the only time Jesus features in the Gospels as a child. He is next described as an adult, about to begin his ministry.

Judea in Jesus' boyhood
Jesus grew up in a world that was dominated by one city, Rome. His own people, the Jews, particularly resented their subjugation by the Romans, whom they regarded as foreign pagans. One significant political event which vividly illustrated Jewish feeling occurred in 6 CE. In this year, Judas the Galilean led a Jewish rebellion against Judea's incorporation into the Roman Empire and the payment of tributes to Rome. The revolt was crushed by the Roman authorities with brutal severity. There is no way of knowing what Jesus thought of these events at the time, but over 20 years later, according to Mark's Gospel, he insisted that people should 'Give to Caesar what is Caesar's and to God what is God's.'

Reverse of the same coin

Judean coin from around the time of Jesus' birth

Herod the Great's Temple, here reconstructed as part of an outdoor scale model of Jerusalem, played a central role in Jesus' early life. Luke narrates how he was taken here as a newborn baby and recognized as the Messiah by two independent witnesses. Luke also tells the story of Jesus as a child discussing the Law with the teachers here. Later in his life Jesus would come into conflict with Jewish elders about the presence of traders and moneychangers in the Temple precincts.

Jesus' family visited Jerusalem every year to celebrate the Feast of the Passover. On their way home one year, when Jesus was 12, they realized that the boy was missing. In great anxiety they returned to the city to look for him. The 12th-century Swiss painting (above) shows the scene when they eventually found him – in the Temple, debating learnedly on Jewish Law.

The lush hills of Galilee where Jesus grew up. This northern province of Israel was far removed from the hustle and bustle of the great city of Jerusalem, 120km (80 miles) to the south in Judea, where Jesus would end his ministry. Jesus often referred to elements of Galilean rural landscape – its vineyards, figtrees, flowers, fields, and wildlife – in his parables and other teachings.

Nazareth, Jesus' childhood home, remained relatively secluded for centuries, despite its closeness to some of the main trade routes through the country. Nestling in a high valley at the southern end of the Lebanon mountain range, with steep hills to the north, west, and east, including the rounded dome of Mount Tabor, it was far removed from the main center of Jewish religious

and political life, Jerusalem. Early in the 20th century Nazareth was still a small rural town (above left). Latterly, Nazareth has grown rapidly (above) and it now has a population of about 60,000 inhabitants. It also has the largest cathedral in the Middle East – the Cathedral of the Annunciation – but even so, Nazareth still retains the feel of an old small town.

John baptizes his cousin Jesus on this font decoration

When Jesus was about 30 years old he left his home town of Nazareth to embark upon his ministry. But prior to this he had to undergo two profound and contrasting rites of passage: baptism by his cousin John, and temptation in the desert and elsewhere by the devil.

Traditionally, baptism was a rite reserved purely to mark the entry of non-Jews, who had turned to Judaism, into the Jewish community. However, John the Baptist – a stern, ascetic figure who lived a frugal existence – began to cause a stir by baptizing Jews and non-Jews alike, telling people to repent, and announcing that a new world order was about to be inaugurated by the Messiah, whose coming was imminent.

■ And a voice came from heaven, 'You are my Son, the beloved; with you I am well pleased.'

Mark 1:11

John baptized people in the River Jordan, near the rocky desert area known as the Wilderness of Judea. When Jesus came to the river and asked to be baptized, John immediately recognized him as the Messiah and hesitated, believing that the Messiah had no need of repentance and baptism. But Jesus argued that it was God's will, so John agreed, baptizing him by total immersion in the river. As Jesus emerged from the water he received divine confirmation of his status when the Holy Spirit descended upon him like a dove and a voice from heaven announced that he was God's beloved son, with whom God was well pleased.

Temptation in the Wilderness
After the sublime moment of baptism and divine revelation, Jesus was immediately led by the Holy Spirit to the desert to be 'tempted,' or tested, by the devil. This desert is usually identified as the Wilderness of Judea itself, which stretched eastward from Jerusalem to the Dead Sea and the River Jordan. This desolate area was, according to popular belief, the abode of demons. Here Jesus fasted for 40 days and 40 nights until he was weak with hunger. At this point the devil appeared and tempted him by saying if he was hungry and was truly the son of God then he should turn desert stones into loaves of bread. But Jesus rebuked him, saying that people needed not just bread to live but also the word of God.

Then the devil took Jesus to the parapet of the Temple in Jerusalem and told him to jump off it, quoting the Scriptures as proof that God would send angels to prevent him from being injured. But Jesus refused to comply, insisting that it was wrong to put God to the test.

Finally, the devil took Jesus to an unnamed mountain from where he could see all the kingdoms of the world. These the devil promised to give to Jesus if only he would worship him. Jesus refused, exclaiming that it was right to worship and serve only God. Defeated, the devil left, and Jesus was then tended to by angels. He was now fully prepared to begin his ministry.

The baptism of Christ depicted in an early mosaic. Jesus, in the center, is being baptized by his cousin John. At the moment of his baptism the Holy Spirit, in the form of a dove, descended upon him from heaven and a voice was heard proclaiming that Jesus was the Son of God.

Baptism and Temptation
The location of Jesus' baptism is controversial, but tradition generally favors El-Maghtas, to the south of Jericho. It was near here, in Qumran, that the strict religious sect known as the Essenes lived, perhaps including John the Baptist among their number. Jesus' later temptation took place in the Wilderness of Judea.

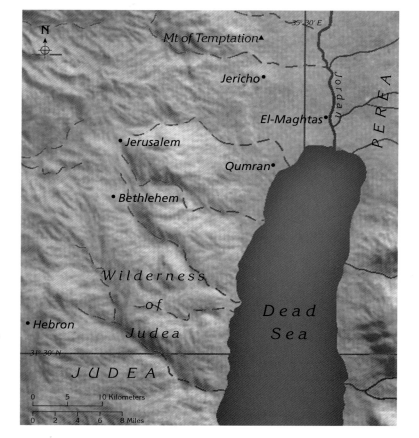

The Essenes

John the Baptist's practice of using ritual immersion to baptize, his asceticism, and some of his teachings have led scholars to suggest he was a member of the Essene sect. This was an austere Jewish group that lived at Qumran to the northwest of the Dead Sea, the very area where John was preaching and baptizing. Excavations at Qumran have revealed communal rooms, a refectory, a scriptorium – where Essene scholars copied sacred texts – as well as stables and a pottery. Writing tools, such as this inkpot (right), have also been found.

The Essenes practiced a strict asceticism, sharing their worldly goods with all fellow believers, and sharing meals. They believed that they were the true followers of God, and their priests claimed to be the descendants of Zadok, a High Priest during the reign of David. This gave them greater authority than the 'false priesthood,' as they called it, of contemporary Judaism.

The Essenes believed that the end of the world was near, and were thus very anxious to stay mentally, spiritually, and physically pure. The last of these concerns is borne out by the many baths and reservoirs found at Qumran.

The settlement of the Essenes at Qumran was well supplied with water. This was brought from the hills by an aqueduct, and then piped to a number of reservoirs and irrigation channels. Near the aqueduct was a bath, which each man used for ritual purification several times a day.

One of the caves in the hills surrounding Qumran where the Dead Sea Scrolls lay hidden for nearly 2000 years. The scrolls formed the library of the Essene community at Qumran and may have been moved to the caves for safety around 68 CE at the time of the Jewish rebellion against Rome.

The ancient settlement of Qumran, close to the Dead Sea, is now reduced to ruins. In Jesus' time, this community of Essenes, a strict Jewish sect, would have followed a simple, ascetic lifestyle that included common ownership of property, rigorous religious devotions, and celibacy.

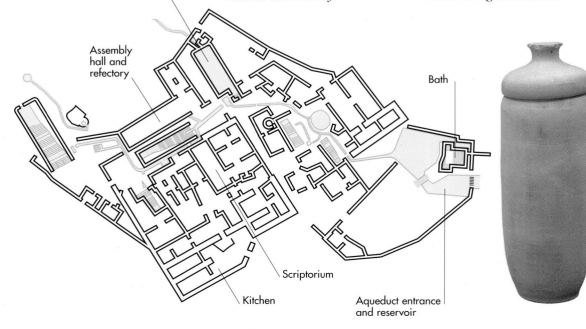

Reservoir

Assembly hall and refectory

Bath

Scriptorium

Kitchen

Aqueduct entrance and reservoir

N

The Dead Sea Scrolls were discovered by accident in 1947 in caves around Qumran. They were made of leather and stored in large clay pots such as the one shown left. The scrolls consisted mainly of religious writings and commentaries.

The Ministry of Jesus

The Gospels record that Jesus made approximately 50 journeys during the three or so years of his ministry. In some cases the places he visited can be identified, but usually the Gospels omit their names or leave the locations vague.

Although Jesus made excursions to Jerusalem and elsewhere, it was mainly in the northern province of Galilee that he did his teaching and healing, and where he recruited his first disciples. According to Josephus, the Jewish historian of the 1st century CE, the whole region was lush and fertile, its rich soil producing an abundance of walnut trees, figs, olives, and vines. The area was also 'excellent for crops or cattle and rich in forests of every kind.' The images used in Jesus' stories and parables – fishing, sowing, harvesting, minding

sheep, and tending vineyards – reflect the rich diversity of the Galilean countryside that he knew so well.

At the heart of the region lay the Sea of Galilee, also known as the Lake of Gennesaret, a freshwater lake about 20km (12 miles) long and 13km (8 miles) wide. Jesus focused much of his attention on the towns situated around this sea. His headquarters and second home was at Capernaum on its northwestern shore. At the town of Gennesaret to the south he healed the sick, and at Tabgha he performed the miracle of feeding the multitude with loaves and fishes. In Bethsaida, just a few miles north of the sea, he healed a blind man. Jesus also visited other parts of Galilee, such as Cana, where he turned water into wine at a wedding feast, and Nain, where he raised a widow's son from the dead.

Above: 12th-century painting, from a Swiss church, of Jesus healing a deaf-and-dumb man.
Background: Olive trees flourish in Palestine.
Map: Galilee.

1. The Sea of Galilee.
2. Vineyards south of Bethlehem.
3. The confluence of the River Jordan and the Sea of Galilee.
4. 4th-century mosaic of fishes from a synagogue in Tiberias.

Ptolemais

GALILEE

Cana
Tiberias

Nazareth

Nain

Capernaum

Sea of Galilee

דגל

③

④

Synagogue pillar in Capernaum

According to all four Gospels, a major feature of Jesus' ministry was his ability, through the power of God, to perform miracles. Scholars still debate the authenticity and symbolism of these miracles, and so tend to distinguish between healing miracles (including exorcism) and those that involved the natural world, such as walking on water or stilling a storm.

Two of Jesus' best-known miracles took place on the Sea of Galilee. The first happened when Jesus and his disciples were sailing across the sea and were caught in a storm. The sea is notorious for the squalls which sweep down with sudden ferocity from Mount Hermon and the plateaus to the north. As the waves broke over the sides of

This synagogue in Capernaum may be similar to the one in which Jesus exorcised a man possessed by an evil spirit.

■ They were filled with great awe and said to one another, 'Who then is this, that even the wind and sea obey him?'

Mark 4:41

the boat, Jesus' companions began to panic, especially when they saw that he was asleep. They woke him and he promptly 'rebuked' the wind and the sea, which at once became calm.

The second miracle on the Sea of Galilee occurred after Jesus had fed a crowd of 5000 people with five loaves of bread and two fishes at a deserted spot nearby. Afterward, Jesus went off alone to pray, and early the next morning the disciples were amazed to see him walking on the surface of the water toward them.

Jesus the healer

Jesus also performed several miracles at Capernaum, including the healing of two paralyzed men. One was the servant of a Roman centurion. The other was a man whose friends lowered him through the roof of the house where Jesus was teaching. Recognizing the strength of their faith, Jesus forgave them for interrupting him and told the man to 'stand up and take your bed and go to your home.'

Some important miracles are only recorded by John's Gospel. These include Jesus' first miracle, when he turned water into wine at a wedding in Cana. But perhaps the most spectacular miracle was the raising of his friend Lazarus from the dead. Jesus ordered that Lazarus' tomb be opened, then shouted to Lazarus to come out. Slowly Lazarus emerged, bound in a corpse's white cloth, having been restored to life after four days in the tomb.

Palestine in Jesus' time
Most of the miracles that Jesus performed took place in his home region of Galilee, although some were performed elsewhere. In Phoenicia, for example, he healed the daughter of a Gentile woman, while in Jerusalem he cured a sick man and restored the sight of a man blind from birth. Crowds traveled long distances to hear Jesus teach – from Judea, Idumea, and lands beyond the River Jordan.

Mediterranean Sea

Dora
Caesarea

SAMARIA
Sama
Syc
Mt Gerizim
Apollonia
Antipatris
Joppa

Lydda
Emmaus
Jericho
Bethabara
Jerusalem Bethphage
Bethany Qumran
Bethlehem
Ascalon

JUDEA

Gaza
Hebron
Machae
Dib

Masada
Beersheba

IDUMAEA

NABATEA

0   10   20 Kilometers
0   10   20 Miles

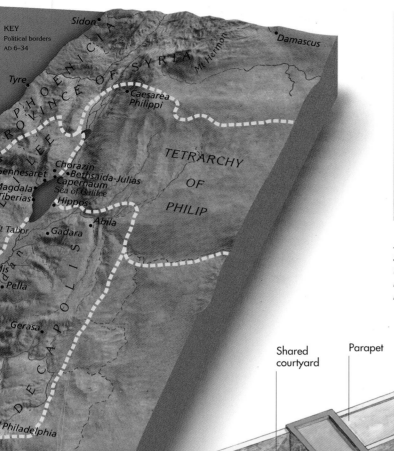

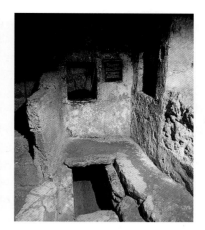

Lazarus' grieving family are seen placing him in the tomb in this medieval painting (above left). Undeterred that Lazarus had been dead for four days,

Jesus ordered Lazarus to rise and leave his tomb. The tomb in Bethany shown in the above photograph is traditionally said to be that of Lazarus himself.

Shared courtyard

Parapet

Flat roof of woven branches coated with clay

Outside stairs

Walls of mud brick coated with plaster

Houses in 1st-century Palestine

In Mark's account of the healing of the paralyzed man at Capernaum, he says that the man's friends dug through the roof of a house to lower him down to Jesus. This was possible because houses of the time often had flat roofs, flimsily made of woven branches coated with clay. Although needing constant maintenance, especially after storms, such flat roofs provided an extra space where people could sleep on hot nights, dry clothes, and ripen fruit or vegetables. Most ordinary houses had one storey, which was often split into two levels: the upper part used for daily living, the lower given over to animals. Light came through the door and small windows, which were set high up in the walls.

In Capernaum, where Jesus performed several miracles, the houses of today's inhabitants look as if they have hardly changed over the last 2000 years.

An Armenian mosaic of a basket of grapes

As Jesus made his way through Palestine he taught the word of God both in public sermons and in private conversations. Often he made his point through parables – stories that use comparisons and examples from everyday life to convey more complex ideas, particularly about faith, ethics, and politics.

The majority of Jesus' parables make a strong, single point, usually calling on people to put their faith in God. In the parable of the prodigal son, for example, a repentant son returns home to his forgiving father after a life of debauchery. Symbolically, this demonstrates God's love for any sinner who returns to him.

■ The kingdom of heaven is like treasure hidden in a field, which someone found and hid; then in his joy he goes and sells all that he has and buys that field.

Matthew 13:44

Complex parables

Some parables, however, had more than one interpretation, which was not always apparent to all of Jesus' listeners. For example, he told a story about a group of wicked tenants who killed their landlord's servants and his son when they came to collect the landlord's share of the crop. When Jesus asked those listening what the landlord should do, they replied fiercely, '... put those wretches to a miserable death, and lease the vineyard to other tenants who will give him the produce at harvest time' (Matthew 21:41). The people understood the message on a personal level, but at another level Jesus was criticizing the religious establishment. Here the landlord

represented God, while the servants represented the prophets; the landlord's son was Jesus himself, and the wicked tenants were the Jewish religious leaders of the day, of whom Jesus was highly critical. These leaders, the high priests and Pharisees, recognized Jesus' criticism of them in this and in other stories. They greatly feared Jesus and his teachings, regarding them as a threat to their authority.

Enduring appeal

The enduring appeal of Jesus' parables owes much to the fact that he took examples from ordinary activities, such as wine-making, farming, and sheep-raising, to illustrate abstract points. One of Jesus' best known parables takes its imagery from farming: a sower scattered seed that fell in various places with different results. Some seed was eaten by birds; some sprang up from rocky soil, but soon withered; some was choked by thorns; and some produced a good crop. The scattered seed symbolizes the Word of God, and the good ground represents receptive listeners who hear, understand, and act upon God's message.

Conversations of Jesus

In John's Gospel, several of Jesus' conversations are recorded in some detail. One of the most engaging of these is his

Jesus used the imagery of sowing and reaping in several parables. Here women reap wheat in Gaza (above) in a way that hasn't changed since Jesus' time. Jesus met the Samaritan woman at a well that probably looked very similar to this one (left). The woman was surprised that Jesus spoke to her because of the ancient hostility between Jews and Samaritans.

Jesus is depicted as the Good Shepherd in this 5th-century mosaic in Ravenna, Italy. Jesus used the everyday image of a shepherd and his sheep to describe his relationship with his followers. Like a good shepherd, he would protect and look after them and would search for any who were lost, rejoicing when they were found.

dialogue with a Samaritan woman at a well. Jesus offered the woman the water of eternal life, and when she professed her faith that the Messiah would come, Jesus replied that he was that very person. Overjoyed, the woman rushed away to tell her people about Jesus. Soon a crowd gathered around him and many became believers. The incident shows that Jesus was prepared to teach everyone, even the Samaritans, whom the Jews ordinarily despised.

The Good Samaritan

One of Jesus' best known parables is the story of the Good Samaritan which he told in response to the question 'And who is my neighbor?' The Samaritan rescued a traveler who had been beaten, robbed, and left for dead on the road to Jericho. Unlike a Jewish priest and a temple official, who walked past the victim on the other side of the road, the Samaritan stopped, bound the man's wounds, and took him to an inn. His action was that of a good neighbor.

For a Jewish audience, the force of the parable stemmed not so much from the behavior of the priest and the official – who feared ritual defilement by touching what they believed to be a corpse – but from the fact that the man who did stop was a Samaritan. Although. in Jesus' time, the Samaritans worshiped the same God as the Jews, and shared some of their religious rituals, the two peoples were traditional enemies. The Jews rejected the Samaritans for their lack of commitment to Jewish Law, while the

Samaritans resented the Jews for destroying their temple on Mount Gerizim. Given this background, the meaning of Jesus' parable is very clear: a good neighbor is someone who overcomes strong emotions, such as hatred and prejudice, to respond to humanitarian needs.

A modern-day shepherd watches over his flock in the hills around Bethlehem. Sheep and shepherds are mentioned over 300 times in the Bible.

Mount Gerizim was sacred to the Samaritans. They never forgave the Jews for destroying their temple on top of the mountain (above) in 128 BCE.

The road from Jerusalem to Jericho passes through the Wilderness of Judea. It was on this inhospitable road that Jesus set the parable of the Good Samaritan.

Sermon on the Mount

Matthew's Gospel tells how one day Jesus led his disciples up a mountainside. Here he sat and delivered to them what has become known as the Sermon on the Mount. Although many scholars now believe the sermon to be a compilation of Jesus' teachings, it is possible that he did deliver a lengthy discourse on one particular occasion.

Tradition identifies the Mount with a grassy hillside that overlooks the Sea of Galilee between Capernaum and Gennesaret. This idyllic spot is now crowned with the Church of the Beatitudes.

The sermon is set out in five sections in Matthew's Gospel, and details the tenets of morality on which Christian teaching is pinned. It begins with the Beatitudes, which state that certain groups of people,

such as those who mourn, who seek peace, who are meek, merciful, or pure in heart, or who have been persecuted for their belief, are blessed by God. Taken together, the Beatitudes paint a picture of the ideal disciple, contrasting aspects of his or her character with the qualities approved by the outside world.

The sermon goes on to examine the relationship between Jesus' teaching and the Jewish Law, which Jesus makes clear he has come to fulfil, not to abolish. He refers to ethical issues such as murder, adultery, and divorce, emphasizing the importance of inner attitude as much as outer action. Jesus urges his followers to be forgiving and to love their enemies. The third section outlines the demands of pious living, particularly almsgiving, prayer, and fasting, while the fourth enjoins people to trust in God. The sermon ends with the parable of the wise man who built his house on rock, to illustrate the power of true belief as a foundation for life.

Above: The Sermon on the Mount, in a fresco from Florence.
Background: The Church of the Beatitudes overlooking the Sea of Galilee.

Map: Possible location of the Sermon on the Mount between Capurnaum and Gennesaret.
1. Springtime in Galilee.
2. Fields of flowers in Galilee.

Capernaum

Gennesaret

Tiberias

Sea of
Galilee

2

1

Easter scene carved on a stone capital

Jesus ended his ministry in Galilee and set out toward Jerusalem on what was to be his final journey. The actual route that Jesus took is unclear as the Gospels give different accounts. Matthew and Mark suggest that he traveled through Judea and crossed the Jordan into the district of Perea, which was at the time under the jurisdiction of Herod Antipas. Luke indicates that Jesus took the usual pilgrim route south from Galilee through Samaria – the same route his parents had taken on their way to Bethlehem before Jesus' birth. Whatever the case, these three Gospels agree that Jesus reached Jericho before proceeding on to Jerusalem in time for the Passover, an important festival time when thousands of pilgrims would be visiting the city for prayer and celebration.

The transfiguration

The event that marks the transition from Jesus' Galilean ministry to his journey to the cross was the transfiguration. Jesus led Peter, John, and James, his three closest disciples, up a 'high mountain.' There he was transfigured into a being of unearthly light, his face shining like the sun, and was joined

■ The next day the great crowd that had come to the festival heard that Jesus was coming to Jerusalem. So they took branches of palm trees and went out to meet him.

John 12:12-13

by two great figures from Israel's past: Moses, representing the Jewish Law, and Elijah, representing Israel's prophets. Elijah also symbolized divine triumph over death, since he had been taken directly up into heaven without dying in this world. A voice then rang out from a cloud, 'This is my Son, the beloved; with him I am well pleased; listen to him.' These words echoed those heard when Jesus was baptized, and which had earlier confirmed his divine status.

The disciples were terrified of the vision but Jesus comforted them and instructed them to tell no one what had happened. As they were returning down the mountain, Jesus told his disciples that the 'Son of Man' – a title he used of himself – was soon to suffer at the hands of his enemies.

Onward to Jerusalem

Aware of what lay ahead of him, Jesus continued his journey south, teaching and preaching along the way. He drove a demon from a young boy and in Perea he told a rich man – to the man's dismay – that he should sell all he had and give the proceeds to the poor. In Jericho he restored the sight of a blind beggar, Bartimaeus, as a reward for his faith.

From Jericho, Jesus traveled southwest toward Jerusalem. As he neared the city, he sent two of his disciples on ahead to

The Golden Gate stands in the eastern wall of Temple Mount. Christian tradition says that Jesus will enter the Holy City by this gate on Judgment Day, so it was bricked up by Muslims after the Crusader period.

River Jordan   Jericho

Jerusalem

The Mount of Temptation (left) is in the wilderness outside Jericho. According to tradition, this is where Jesus, at the start of his ministry, fasted for 40 days and nights and resisted the devil's temptations. Now, on his final journey, he passed this way again and may once more have faced temptation – this time of escaping the terrible fate awaiting him in Jerusalem.

This mosaic map (right) was found in 1896 in the Byzantine Church of St George in the ancient city of Madaba in Jordan. The map dates from 560 CE and is annotated in Greek with explanations and biblical texts. It would have originally measured 22 x 7m (70 x 22 ft) but has since been damaged by vandalism and building works. The surviving part, 5 x 10m (16 x 35 ft), is made up of two million colored pieces and shows the Holy Land from the Dead Sea to the Mediterranean.

collect a donkey (or colt) that would be waiting for him. Jesus mounted the donkey and rode toward the city gate. People came out of their houses and thronged the wayside to welcome him, shouting 'Hosanna!' and spreading their cloaks and palm branches on the road.

In this way, the Gospels depict Jesus' arrival in Jerusalem as fulfilling the Old Testament prophecies of a Messiah coming to his people in triumph. But his choice of a donkey as his mount, rather than a horse, indicated that he had come as a peaceful and humble Messiah, not as a warrior Messiah, ready to lead an uprising and drive the Romans from the land, that most Jews expected and wanted.

Even so, Jesus' triumphant arrival served to fan the flames of expectation in the city, which was already buzzing with festive excitement. More ominously, it also agitated some of the Jewish elders who were growing increasingly concerned about the adulation that Jesus was inspiring.

Mounts Hermon and Tabor *have both been identified as the 'high mountain' on which Jesus' transfiguration took place. Mount Hermon (above left) lies about 45km (30 miles) to the northeast of the Sea of Galilee, and rises to 2750m (9000 ft). Mount Tabor (above right) stands alone in the valley* *of Jezreel, some 16km (10 miles) southwest of the Sea of Galilee, and rises to 411m (1350 ft). Atop Mount Tabor stands the Church of the Transfiguration, but Mount Hermon has the better claim as the actual site, being nearer to Bethsaida-Julias which was Jesus' last named stop before his transfiguration.*

Bethabara, where John the Baptist lived and baptized

Gethsemane, where Christ was betrayed

Dead Sea

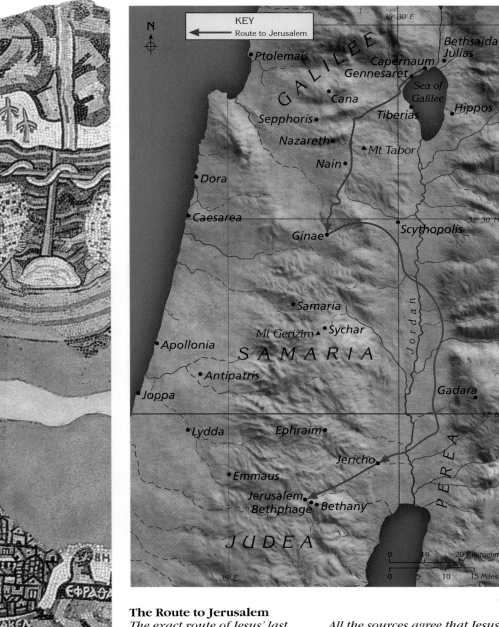

The Route to Jerusalem
The exact route of Jesus' last journey is unknown. This map is based on the accounts in the Gospels of Matthew and Mark.

All the sources agree that Jesus went to Jericho before proceeding to Jerusalem in time for the Passover festival.

A street in the Old City of Jerusalem

Nestling in the hills of Judea's Central Highlands, the city of Jerusalem first entered Jewish history when it was captured from the Canaanites by King David in the early 10th century BCE. By Jesus' time it was firmly established as the spiritual and political center of the Jewish world. It was the focus for thousands of pilgrims at the Passover, and other major festivals, to come and worship and perform rituals at the Temple.

During the reign of Herod the Great (37–4 BCE), when Judea was part of the Roman Empire, much of the city was rebuilt and embellished with new buildings, including sumptuous baths, an amphitheater, and a hippodrome. The city's walls were strengthened and a magnificent fortress – named Antonia after Herod's ally, the Roman general Mark Antony – was raised above the northwest corner of Temple Mount. In the Upper City, on Jerusalem's west side, Herod constructed a luxurious new palace.

Away from these imposing civic structures, the bulk of Jerusalem's population – estimated at 250,000 – lived in humble one- or two-storey dwellings built around courtyards and connected by narrow winding streets, suited more to donkeys and mules than to wheeled vehicles. Sanitation was basic, with street gutters serving as conduits for human and other waste. Water was taken manually from public reservoirs – such as the ancient Pool of Siloam and the Sheep's Pools, situated on the edge of the city – and carried to local cisterns. As well as small specialist shops, such as jewelers, cobblers, and metalworkers, there were several twice-weekly markets devoted to particular goods and products, including wood, wool, cattle, clothing, and foodstuffs.

The Temple

Jerusalem's most impressive and sacred structure was the Temple, which Herod began to renovate and enlarge around 20 BCE. Building work continued until just before the Temple's final destruction by the Romans in 70 CE. The Temple was built on the site of two previous temples on top of a huge artificial mound. The entire complex – at the time the largest religious complex in the Western World – comprised several courtyards enclosing the main sanctuary, within which was the Holy of Holies or Most Holy Place housing the Ark of the Covenant. The buildings were decorated with gold and beautiful stones. Flavius Josephus, the Jewish historian, described the Temple, when viewed from afar, as gleaming like a mountain covered with snow.

Antonia Fortress

Temple area

A plan of Jerusalem from a Byzantine mosaic known as the Madaba Map. This rather stylized representation shows the Temple, the Antonia Fortress, and Golgotha, where Jesus was crucified.

Church of the Holy Sepulchre (on Golgotha)

Herod's palace

Essenes' Gate

Kidron Valley

Pool of Siloam

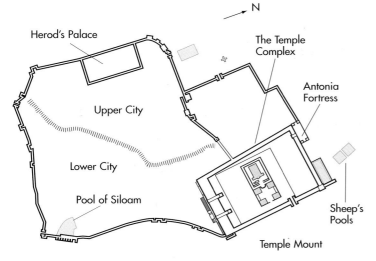

The groundplan of Jerusalem above shows the probable line of the city walls around the time of Jesus' death. The plan also features the major

building projects carried out by Herod the Great – his palace, the Antonia Fortress, and, most ambitious of all, the Temple, which dominated the city.

Temple Mount, the site of Herod's magnificent Temple, is today graced by the Dome of the Rock, an Islamic shrine that marks the spot from where the prophet Mohammed is said to have ascended into heaven.

The Western Wall (below) is all that remains of the Temple ramparts. It is popularly known as the 'Wailing Wall,' because Jews are said to have gathered there to mourn ever since the Temple's destruction.

Herod the Great's Jerusalem
This reconstruction of the city of Jerusalem is based on archeological evidence and the writings of Flavius Josephus, the Jewish historian. The city that Jesus knew had been largely constructed by Herod the Great, appointed King of the Jews by his Roman masters in 37 BCE. In order to ingratiate himself with the people, who resented Roman occupation, Herod embarked upon an ambitious building program, and under his rule Jerusalem prospered. By Jesus' time, Jerusalem, dominated by Herod's massive Temple, was one of the most impressive cities in Rome's eastern empire.

Hebrew coin showing the entrance to the Temple

Soon after his triumphal entry into Jerusalem, Jesus caused an uproar in the Temple by forcibly expelling the dovesellers and moneychangers who operated there in the Court of the Gentiles.

As a result, his notoriety and his appeal to the public spread rapidly. Jesus' action, combined with his overt criticism of the religious establishment, increased the resentment and fear of him already felt among the higher Jewish authorities. As the controversy surrounding Jesus increased, the high priests began to plot his downfall.

A short while after the incident in the Temple, Jesus went to Bethany, just outside Jerusalem, to visit a man named Simon the Leper. While he was there, an unnamed woman came to him and anointed his head with an expensive perfume, prompting the other guests to accuse her of wastefulness. Jesus, however, defended the woman's action; she was, he said, simply preparing him for his burial − an open reference to his impending fate.

This building is thought to be the one in which the Last Supper was held. When the disciples asked Jesus where they would have their Passover meal, Jesus instructed them to go into the city, where they would meet a man carrying a jug of water. The man took the disciples to a house where they found an upper room furnished in readiness for the meal. It was at this occasion that Jesus warned the disciples that one of them would betray him to the Jewish authorities.

■ Woe to that one by whom the Son of Man is betrayed! It would have been better for that one not to have been born.

Mark 14:21

The Last Supper

Two days later, Jesus and his 12 disciples gathered in the upstairs room of a house in Jerusalem to eat the Passover supper. This was to be the last meal they would take together. Before the meal Jesus washed the disciples' feet to illustrate that all men are equal in the sight of God. While they were eating, Jesus announced to their consternation that one among them would betray him. The guilty man was Judas Iscariot, who had secretly agreed to hand Jesus over to the Jewish authorities for 30 pieces of silver.

After issuing these words of foreboding, Jesus took some bread, blessed it, and then broke it and gave the pieces to his disciples, saying that it was his body. He then blessed a cup of wine and passed it round for everyone to drink from. As each did so, he proclaimed that it was the 'blood of the covenant', which had been 'poured out for many.' In this way, Jesus established the ritual of the Eucharist, or Holy Communion, which allows believers to partake in his sacrificial death. The Eucharist also allows them to share in a new relationship with God, not based on the old Law given to the Israelites, but on the new Law established by God's love for all humanity.

Once the supper was over, Jesus and his disciples made their way across the city to Gethsemane on the Mount of Olives, a place to the east of Jerusalem where they often went to pray and rest. Here, in the peace of an olive grove, Jesus was to contemplate his final hours.

The Cleansing of the Temple

Shortly after Jesus' triumphant entry into Jerusalem, he went to the Temple and drove out the people trading there. He then threw over the tables of moneychangers and dovesellers (right). The authorities viewed these traders as essential to the running of the Temple. Doves were required for sacrifices, while the moneychangers converted ordinary currency into the special Temple coinage with which Jews were required to buy their sacrificial animals and to pay their annual Temple tax. Although these traders operated legally, Jesus' dramatic action was intended as a protest against the materialistic and commercial atmosphere that their activities had created in the Temple, something that Jesus felt was completely inappropriate to a place of prayer and worship.

Jesus may also have been angry that non-Jews were barred from worshiping in the Court of the Gentiles, which was the only part of the Temple open to them. This ran counter to Jesus' mission, in fulfillment of the Old Testament prophets, to bring salvation to Jews and Gentiles alike so that all might worship in the Temple together without distinction.

The Last Supper

The final meal shared by Jesus and his disciples has inspired artists for centuries. In this 12th-century wall painting from the monastery of Asinou on the island of Cyprus, Jesus is seated on the left, crowned with a halo. The grey-haired man with the halo on the right is Simon Peter, while Judas Iscariot is probably the leaning figure with his arm outstretched.

Gethsemane

Having shared his last meal with the disciples, Jesus led them out of Jerusalem to the Mount of Olives, a small hill across the Kidron Valley, overlooking the eastern walls of the city. Here Jesus prepared himself for his imminent ordeal.

Mark's Gospel recounts that once they arrived at the Mount, Jesus turned to Peter and told him that he would deny him three times before morning. Horrified, Peter and the rest of the disciples assured Jesus that they would never betray him so. They then went down to Gethsemane – which means 'oil press' in Hebrew – an orchard or garden lying toward the bottom of the hill. According to John's Gospel, Jesus and his disciples had gathered here several times before. Jesus told his disciples to sit and wait while he took Peter, John, and

James a short distance away to pray. Then, in a heartfelt moment of intimacy, Jesus told these three closest companions his deep sorrow at his impending fate and asked them to stay awake while he went to pray.

He then walked off, prostrated himself on the ground, and, in a moment that proved that even he was subject to temptation and human frailty, asked God to spare him the ordeal he was about to face. Almost immediately he retracted his plea, saying that God's will was also his will. Even in his moment of greatest distress Jesus was prepared to accept the path God had set out for him.

When Jesus returned to his three disciples, he found them fast asleep, just when he needed their support most. Jesus chided them and twice more went off to pray, returning each time to find them asleep. As Jesus spoke to the disciples for the third time, Judas suddenly appeared with an armed mob to arrest him. In an act of supreme irony, Judas identified Jesus to his persecutors by kissing him, and Jesus was taken away.

Above: Jesus praying at Gethsemane, in a painting from Siena, Italy.
Background: Gethsemane viewed from the Mount of Olives.
Map: Jerusalem and Gethsemane.

1. Path from Gethsemane to Mount Zion.
2. Judas betrays Jesus with a kiss.
3. Church of All Nations at Gethsemane at night.
4. Jesus and his disciples.

Temple

Gethsemane

Mount of
Olives

Walls of Jerusalem

4

3

Carving of a menorah – a Jewish
candlestick and symbol of faith

Following his arrest in Gethsemane Jesus was taken to face the Sanhedrin – the Jews' ruling council – at the house of Caiaphas, the High Priest. Jerusalem's religious leaders had become increasingly frightened that what Jesus had been teaching would undermine their authority. They also feared that his popularity with the people would increase the ever-present unrest among the people, placing a further strain on relations between them and the Romans.

Many false witnesses were brought forward to give evidence against Jesus, but their stories conflicted. They made wild accusations, claiming, for instance, that Jesus had said he would destroy the Temple and rebuild it in three days,

■ Then Pilate took Jesus and had him flogged. And the soldiers wove a crown of thorns and put it on his head, and they dressed him in a purple robe.

John 19:1–2

misinterpreting a reference that Jesus had made to his own death and resurrection. Throughout all of these proceedings, Jesus remained silent. Then Caiaphas asked Jesus directly whether he was the Christ. At this point, according to Mark, Jesus replied 'I am' – although in Matthew and Luke's accounts his reply is ambiguous. This was enough for Caiaphas, and he accused Jesus of blasphemy. Realizing they could do nothing without Roman authority, the Sanhedrin had Jesus brought before Pontius Pilate, the Roman procurator.

Jesus before Pilate and Herod

The Sanhedrin had no power to impose the death penalty, even for blasphemy. In order to make sure that Jesus was executed, they had to convince Pilate that Jesus was guilty of treason, which was indeed a capital offense under Roman law. Pilate listened while the chief priests made their accusations and was astonished that Jesus made no reply. The implication in all four Gospels is that Pilate was not convinced of Jesus' guilt. In Luke's version, Pontius Pilate, on hearing that Jesus was from Galilee, which fell under the jurisdiction of the Roman vassal king Herod Antipas, sent him to Herod for his opinion. When Herod questioned Jesus he too was unable to find any solid evidence against him, despite the vehement accusations of the chief priests. After subjecting him to mockery and ridicule, Herod sent Jesus back to Pilate.

According to the Gospels, Pilate remained loath to condemn Jesus and, in a final attempt to avoid passing judgment, publicly offered to release him as an act of good will customarily made at the Passover festival. But the crowd that had gathered outside Pilate's headquarters called instead for the release of another prisoner, Barabbas. This man, who was probably a Zealot – a Jewish independence fighter – had been thrown into prison on suspicion of insurrection and murder. Fearing a riot if he didn't comply with the crowd's wishes, Pilate reluctantly released Barabbas. Symbolically washing his hands of the affair, he then gave orders for Jesus to be scourged and taken away for crucifixion.

The court of the Gentiles was the only part of the Temple that was open to non-Jews. This inscription, one of several in the Temple, warned anyone who was not a Jew against venturing any further.

Outer
Courtyard

Royal
Porch

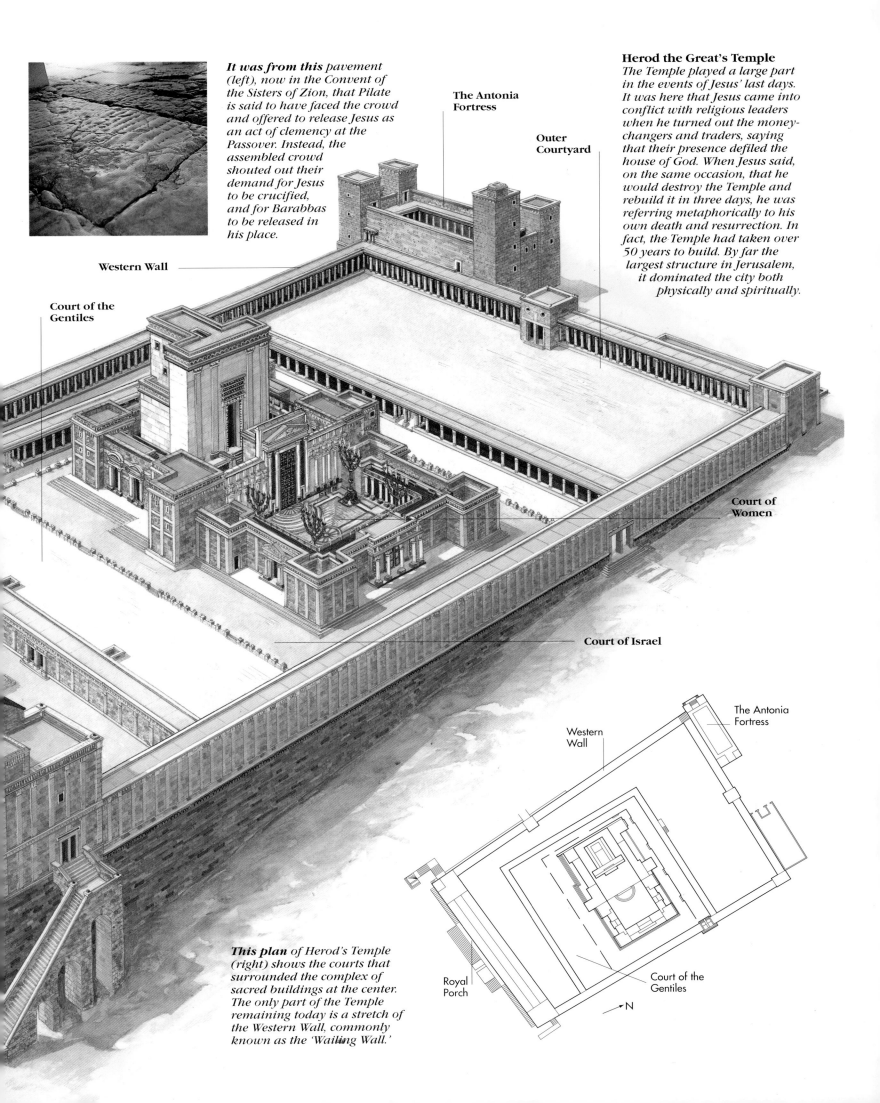

It was from this pavement (left), now in the Convent of the Sisters of Zion, that Pilate is said to have faced the crowd and offered to release Jesus as an act of clemency at the Passover. Instead, the assembled crowd shouted out their demand for Jesus to be crucified, and for Barabbas to be released in his place.

The Antonia Fortress

Outer Courtyard

Western Wall

Court of the Gentiles

Herod the Great's Temple

The Temple played a large part in the events of Jesus' last days. It was here that Jesus came into conflict with religious leaders when he turned out the money-changers and traders, saying that their presence defiled the house of God. When Jesus said, on the same occasion, that he would destroy the Temple and rebuild it in three days, he was referring metaphorically to his own death and resurrection. In fact, the Temple had taken over 50 years to build. By far the largest structure in Jerusalem, it dominated the city both physically and spiritually.

Court of Women

Court of Israel

This plan of Herod's Temple (right) shows the courts that surrounded the complex of sacred buildings at the center. The only part of the Temple remaining today is a stretch of the Western Wall, commonly known as the 'Wailing Wall.'

The Antonia Fortress

Western Wall

Royal Porch

Court of the Gentiles

→ N

After he had been sentenced to death by Pontius Pilate, Jesus was led away and flogged by Roman soldiers, who then jeeringly dressed him in a purple cloak, placed a crown of thorns on his head, and hailed him as 'king of the Jews'. Although he was severely weakened by the scourging, Jesus was forced to carry the heavy beam that would form the horizontal bar of his cross, and made to walk along the street that led outside the city walls to Golgotha, the place where criminals were regularly executed.

Jesus being helped by Simon of Cyrene

Jesus' path to Golgotha cannot now be traced, but during the 13th century the Christian Crusaders occupying Jerusalem established a possible route. This led from the site of the Antonia Fortress westward through the streets to the Church of the Holy Sepulcher, believed to have been built on the hill of Golgotha. A product of piety rather than history, it became known as the 'Via Dolorosa,' the 'Way of Sorrows.'

The Via Dolorosa
As Jesus staggered painfully toward the site of his execution at Golgotha, several incidents occurred that were later commemorated in the 14 Stations of the Cross, numbered on the illustration of Jerusalem below. Some incidents are recorded in the Gospels; others have been derived from pious tradition.

1. Jesus is condemned to be crucified at the Antonia Fortress 2. Jesus picks up his cross after being scourged by the soldiers 3. Weakened by his scourging, Jesus falls for the first time 4. Jesus meets his mother, Mary 5. Jesus is helped to carry the cross by Simon of Cyrene 6. Veronica wipes the sweat and blood from Jesus' face 7. Jesus falls for the second time 8. Jesus consoles the women of Jerusalem 9. Jesus falls under his burden for the third time 10. Arriving at Golgotha, Jesus is stripped of his clothes 11. Jesus is nailed to the cross and placed between two robbers 12. Jesus dies 13. Jesus is taken from the cross and put into his mother's arms 14. Jesus' body is laid to rest in the tomb of Joseph of Arimathea and a heavy stone is rolled across the entrance.

The traditional route of the Via Dolorosa is based on the premise that Jesus was tried at the Antonia Fortress. Some scholars now believe that his trial took place at Herod's palace and have suggested a different route, which is shown on the city plan at right.

N

Antonia Fortress

Golgotha

Temple Mount

Herod's palace

Traditional route ___ Probable route ___

This stone relief, above the doorway of the Armenian Catholic Church of the Spasm, marks the fourth station. It records the moment when Jesus met his mother, Mary – an event that is not

mentioned by any of the Gospel writers. By tradition, it fulfils the prophecy of Simeon, who met the holy family soon after Jesus was born and predicted that he would cause Mary great grief.

St Stephen's Gate is situated at the eastern end of the city, beyond the Antonia Fortress. It was also known as the Lion's Gate, because of the lions carved on either side of the arch.

The Monastery of the Flagellation is located close to the site of the Antonia Fortress. It marks the start of the Via Dolorosa, which is walked by many thousands of pilgrims today.

The many streets that lead off the Via Dolorosa have probably changed little in appearance since the time of Christ, despite the frequent rebuilding of Jerusalem over the centuries.

The Ecce Homo arch is identified in Christian tradition as the place where Pilate showed Jesus to the Jews with the words: 'Behold the Man'. The third station of the cross lies under the arch.

John's Gospel states that Pilate's trial of Jesus occurred at 'the judge's seat at a place known as the Stone Pavement.' This pavement is said to form part of the floor of the Convent of the Sisters of Zion.

A stone relief marks the third station of the cross. Although the event is not recorded by the Gospels, popular tradition holds that Jesus fell here for the first time, wearied by his burden.

The eighth station of the cross is marked by a stone carved with the letters 'NIKA,' which means 'Jesus Christ conquers.' It was here that Jesus consoled the women of Jerusalem.

The Church of the Holy Sepulcher is said to have been built over Golgotha – where Jesus was crucified – and over his tomb. The final five stations of the cross are located inside the church.

Jesus carries his cross, as shown in a 14th-century manuscript

Jesus was led from Pilate's palace to Golgotha, 'The Place of the Skull,' and executed by crucifixion, the harshest punishment in Roman law. It was 9 o'clock in the morning when Jesus was raised up on the cross between two convicted thieves who were also being crucified. As the soldiers went about their work, Jesus begged God to forgive them, saying that they did not realize what they were doing. The soldiers then divided up Jesus' clothes among themselves, casting lots for the last garment. On the crosses they fixed notices stating the men's crimes. In Jesus' case, the notice read simply 'The King of the Jews.'

As he hung on the cross, suffering excruciating physical and spiritual pain, Jesus was mocked by passers-by, and by some of his opponents, who taunted him to save himself if he

> ■ When they came to the place that is called The Skull, they crucified Jesus there with the criminals.
>
> Luke 23:33

really was the son of God. Even one of the robbers hanging beside him joined in the insults, though the other rebuked him, reminding him that Jesus had committed no crime.

Death of Jesus
At midday, a darkness fell over the land and lasted for three hours. According to John, during these hours Jesus' agony on the cross was witnessed by his mother, his aunt, and Mary Magdalene, as well as by one of the disciples, probably John. Jesus spoke to Mary and the disciple exhorting them to look after each other. Luke says Jesus also comforted the friendly robber, who begged Jesus to remember him in heaven.

As the end of his suffering drew near Matthew and Mark report that Jesus cried out '*Eloi, Eloi, lema sabachthani?*' meaning 'My God, my God, why have you forsaken me?' Mark and John go on to say that on hearing this one of the bystanders rushed up with a sponge soaked in wine vinegar which he lifted up to Jesus' lips for him to drink. According to John, Jesus then uttered his final words – 'It is finished' – and died. At that moment the curtain in the Temple separating the Holy of Holies from the rest of the sanctuary was ripped in two, the earth shook and rocks were split apart. In addition, Matthew says that tombs opened and the bodies of the holy were brought back to life. It was just after 3 o'clock.

Jesus had hung on the cross for only six hours. Victims of crucifixion could take two or more days to die, and the soldiers were surprised that Jesus had died so quickly. John reports that one even pierced his side with a spear to check that he was indeed dead, and a mixture of blood and water flowed from the wound. Matthew concludes that the Roman soldiers and the commanding officer who had been guarding Jesus were convinced by his words and his manner of dying that Jesus was truly the Son of God.

The burial
After Jesus' death, a rich man named Joseph of Arimathea, who was a member of the Jewish council, the Sanhedrin, but who had also been a secret follower of Jesus, asked Pontius Pilate for permission to bury Jesus in his own tomb. Pilate agreed and Joseph took down the body and wrapped it in linen. John records that he was helped by another Sanhedrin member, Nicodemus, who had secretly visited Jesus to hear his teachings. Nicodemus brought perfumes to anoint the body and Joseph placed Jesus in the tomb, newly cut out of the rock. These events were witnessed by Jesus' grieving mother and, Luke says, by several other women. They then watched from a distance as Joseph rolled a large stone across the entrance to seal the tomb.

Pontius Pilate
During Jesus' time, the Roman province of Judea fell under the procuratorship of Pontius Pilate. Appointed by Emperor Tiberius in 26 CE Pilate held the post for about 10 years. The coins shown above were struck during his rule.

Pilate was not a popular figure. Not only did he represent the authority of Rome, but he was also dismissive of Jewish rights and customs and was happy to use violent methods to keep his subjects under control. Little is known of Pilate, but to have acquired the rank of procurator he is likely to have come from a good Roman family. The Gospels allow him some credit for his reluctance to condemn Jesus, but his motivation is unclear, and the evidence against Jesus was scant indeed. In any event, despite Pilate's symbolic act of washing his hands of Jesus' blood, his eventual bowing to public pressure – presumably to avoid unrest among his subjects – means that much of the responsibility for the death of Jesus must still lie squarely at his door.

Christ's crucifixion *is perhaps the most compelling of all Christian images. The painted crucifix to the left is the work of the Italian 'Master of St Francis,' who was active around 1260–1270. In the Christian faith, Jesus' death marks the culmination of his mission on earth, his ultimate sacrifice redeeming the sins of humanity and opening the way for salvation. It also fulfilled the prophecy of Isaiah in the Old Testament that the Messiah would be a suffering servant of God and humanity rather than a glorious king.*

The rock tomb *below, sealed with a rolling stone, is similar to the one in which Jesus' body was placed. Wealthy men in Jesus' time would have their tombs built before their death – hence Joseph of Arimathea's offer of his own tomb for Jesus' interment. In the intense heat of the region, it was essential to bury bodies swiftly as decay set in quickly. John's Gospel makes reference to this in his account of the raising of Lazarus from the dead, when Martha warns Jesus of the 'stench,' since Lazarus had already been dead for four days.*

A gruesome relic *from an old crucifixion, this heelbone impaled on a spike was found in a burial jar in Jerusalem. Victims were usually nailed to the cross through their wrists and heels. Nails through the hand would not bear a person's weight unless the arms were also roped to the crossbar. Often the victims' legs would also be broken. Death would eventually come from asphyxiation and exhaustion.*

Byzantine mural showing the resurrected Christ

On the third day after Jesus died, Mary Magdalene went to his tomb, possibly to anoint his body with spices. The Gospels vary in the details they give of the events of that morning. Matthew, Mark, and Luke, for example, record that Mary was accompanied by other women, whereas John reports that she was on her own. On one vital point, however, they agree: the stone that sealed the entrance to the tomb had been moved aside and the body of Jesus was gone.

According to Matthew, an angel told Mary and her companion that Jesus had risen from the dead and would meet them in Galilee. Mark describes the angel as a man in a white robe, while Luke states there were two angels whose clothes gleamed like lightning. John's account is quite different: he says that Mary encountered a figure whom she assumed was the gardener. This man asked her why she was crying and then, to reassure her, he addressed her by her name. In amazement, she suddenly saw that he was Jesus.

Encounters in Galilee

After his resurrection from the dead, Jesus appeared to his disciples on a number of occasions. The form in which he appeared, however, is uncertain. John's Gospel implies that Jesus was able to appear or vanish supernaturally at will, and

■ They found the stone rolled away from the tomb, but when they went in, they did not find the body.

Luke 24:2–3

when Mary Magdalene tried to touch him, Jesus would not allow her to, saying that he had yet to return to his Father. Luke stresses that Jesus was made of flesh and bone, and was not a ghost. Similarly, John tells how Jesus invited the sceptical disciple Thomas to touch his wounds to dispel any doubts about his physical reality.

Both Luke and John tell of other appearances of Jesus in some detail. In one episode, Luke describes how two disciples were walking to the village of Emmaus, a short distance from Jerusalem, when Jesus joined them on their journey. But the two men did not recognize that their new companion was Jesus until later, when he blessed and broke some bread at supper. In an instant they realized who their companion was, but, at that moment, Jesus disappeared from their sight.

A later appearance of Jesus is related by John. Peter and six companions were fishing without success on the Sea of Galilee. A mysterious figure on the shore called out to them to cast their nets from the right side of their boat. They did so, and were amazed to find their net soon bulging with fish. The disciples then realized that the mysterious figure was Jesus, and Peter rushed to the shore to greet him. This, John says, was the third time that Jesus appeared to his disciples after he rose from the dead.

Jesus instructs his disciples

Apart from proving that he had risen from the dead, Jesus appeared to the disciples to instruct them in their future duties. He ordered them to go and preach his teachings throughout the world. Peter was singled out for even greater responsibility: leadership of the disciples as well as the growing numbers of Jesus' other followers.

Jesus eventually left the disciples by being miraculously raised to heaven – an event known as the Ascension. Luke describes how Jesus appeared to the disciples for the last time, blessed them, and was taken up into heaven. Yet Jesus remained spiritually with the disciples, for Mark adds that they received signs that the Lord was working with them.

Jesus emerges from the tomb (above) as the soldiers who were guarding the entrance sleep on. The soldiers were posted there on Pilate's orders after a request from the Jewish chief priests, who were afraid that Jesus' body would be stolen by his disciples to fulfil his promise to rise from the dead on the third day.

The resurrection of Jesus holds out the promise of both resurrection and eternal life for all believers. This 11th-century Byzantine church mosaic shows the resurrected Christ extending his hand to help a man climb from his tomb at the Day of Judgment.

Men still fish on the Sea of Galilee (left) as they did in the days of Peter and Andrew, Jesus' first disciples, whom he said would 'fish for people'. The Byzantine mosaic (far left) shows Jesus with fishermen. After his resurrection, Jesus appeared to some of his disciples who were fishing without success. He called to them from the shore, telling them where to cast their net. They followed his directions and caught a great haul.

Jewish menorahs carved on a column from Corinth

Toward the end of his Gospel, Luke recounts how Jesus reassured the disciples that his death and resurrection fulfilled ancient prophecies. These prophecies also told that the repentance and forgiveness of sins would be preached in Jesus' name to all nations. Jesus then instructed the disciples to stay in Jerusalem after his death, where they would receive power from the Holy Spirit to spread the Gospel. The Holy Spirit is referred to again in the Acts of the Apostles, which recounts how Jesus told the disciples that they would soon receive a baptism, not with water, but with the Spirit.

■ Divided tongues, as of fire, appeared among them, and a tongue rested on each of them.

Acts: 2:3

Almost two months after Jesus' death, at the Jewish Feast of Pentecost, which commemorated Moses' being given the Jewish Law on Mount Sinai, the disciples were gathered in a house in Jerusalem when they heard a rushing wind. Looking about them, they saw tongues of fire flickering above their heads. They were instantly filled with the Holy Spirit, and 'began to speak in other languages.'

Many Jews and Gentile converts from various parts of the Roman Empire were in Jerusalem at this festival time. Alarmed by the noise of the wind, they went to the disciples, and were astonished to hear them speaking in all the different languages of the people gathered there.

The crowd was bewildered and wondered what it all meant; some even said that the disciples were drunk. Peter then addressed the throng and in an inspired speech told them how these strange events had been foretold by the prophet Joel. He reminded them that Jesus had been put to death in spite of the evidence of the miracles, wonders, and signs that showed he was the Son of God. Peter concluded by assuring them that Jesus had been raised from the dead and had received the Holy Spirit, but he also implicated the Jews in causing Jesus' death.

Stirred by Peter's words, many begged to know how to make amends. Peter said to repent and be baptized, and some 3000 converted to the faith there and then. That day the disciples had indeed received from the Holy Spirit the power to preach the Gospel, just as Jesus had promised.

The Temple of Zeus at Cyrene betrays the Greek origins of this city situated on the coast of North Africa. Cyrene was prosperous, with a large Jewish population. Cyrenian Jews were in the crowd to which the disciples, filled with the Holy Spirit, spoke in different languages.

Pentecostal Pilgrims
The Jewish feast of Pentecost, also known as the Feast of Weeks, took place on the 50th day after the Passover. This was a time of the year when Jewish pilgrims would come to Jerusalem from all over the Middle East – indeed, by the time of Jesus, from all over the Roman Empire and beyond – to worship in the Temple. It was at this festival that the disciples received the Holy Spirit and began preaching to the assembled crowds of Pentecostal pilgrims. This map shows the main centers from which the Jews came and the well-established pilgrim routes they would have taken to get to Jerusalem.

Tongues of fire, representing the Holy Spirit, hover over the heads of the apostles in this 11th-century mosaic which decorates the apse of a church in Greece. In the center, the presence of the Holy Spirit is further indicated by a dove, the same form in which it appeared when Jesus was baptized in the River Jordan by his cousin John the Baptist.

Black Sea

Caspian Sea

Persian Gulf

A R A B I A

MACEDONIA
Byzantium
Philippi
Aegean
Sea
Pergamum
Athens
Ephesus
Miletus
Sinope
Heraclea
BITHYNIA
PONTUS
Ancyra
PHRYGIA
Sardis
Iconium
CAPPADOCIA
Tarsus
CYPRUS
Salamis
Antioch
MESOPOTAMIA
Sidon
Tyre
Caesarea
Joppa
Ptolemais
Damascus
Palmyra
Tigris
MEDIA
Ecbatana
PARTHIA
Alexandria
Gaza
Jerusalem
JUDEA
Babylon
Seleucia
Susa
ELAM
Euphrates
Red Sea

KEY
ASIA
Places mentioned in Acts
Border of Roman Empire
Routes of pilgrims

Synagogues, such as these at Sardis in Asia Minor (above), now modern Turkey, and Capernaum (left), on the northern shore of the Sea of Galilee, were the main meeting places for the local Jewish communities. It would have been to centers such as these that the Pentecostal pilgrims, who had witnessed Peter's speech in Jerusalem, would have returned. Here, those who had been convinced by what they had heard and seen could discuss their experiences, passing on the word of Jesus. Groups such as these founded the centers from which the Christian Church spread.

Carving of a lion from St Stephen's Gate, Jerusalem

One of the most significant events in the development of the Christian Church was the conversion of Saul – later known by his Roman name, Paul – to the Christian faith. He was to become a tireless and determined promoter of the word of Jesus, spreading it to the Gentile world of the Roman Empire. Paradoxically, before his conversion, Saul was an ardent devotee of the Jewish Law, and a zealous persecutor of the earliest Christians, whom he saw as a threat to Judaism. He first appears in the Bible as an approving bystander when the disciple Stephen is stoned to death – condemned for blasphemy by the Jews. Saul went on to persecute Christ's followers in Jerusalem. His fateful journey to Damascus, which would lead to his conversion, was made with the express intention of arresting Christians living there.

> ■ He fell to the ground and heard a voice say to him, 'Saul, Saul, why do you persecute me?'
>
> Acts 9:4

Saul set off on the long journey north from Jerusalem to Damascus and as he approached his destination he was suddenly dazzled by a brilliant light. He fell to the ground and heard the voice of Jesus asking why he was persecuting him. Jesus then told Saul to get up, continue his journey to Damascus and there await further instructions. Saul found that he was now blind and had to be led to the city where lodgings were found for him with a man named Judas living in Straight Street. There Saul remained, confused, frightened and sightless, neither eating nor drinking.

Paul's baptism

Three days later, a Christian named Ananias received orders from God to go to Saul and bless him. At once, 'something like scales' fell from Saul's eyes and he regained his sight. He was then baptized into the Church and immediately began to preach the Gospel in the synagogues of Damascus. But his bold approach antagonized some of the Jews in the city. They plotted to kill him and kept watch over the city gates to catch

St Stephen's Gate, or the Lions' Gate (left) forms part of the eastern wall of Jerusalem. According to a late medieval tradition, it was to a spot outside this gate that the disciple Stephen was dragged to be stoned to death. The Bible says that Saul watched Stephen's execution with approval, minding the clothes cast to the ground by those taking part in the stoning.

Damascus, one of the oldest continuously inhabited cities in the world, was founded at an oasis watered by two rivers, known in the Bible as the Abana and the Parphar rivers. Today's city contains many traces of the walled settlement of Saul's day, and there still exists a thoroughfare called Straight Street (left). Saul took lodgings here on his arrival in the city.

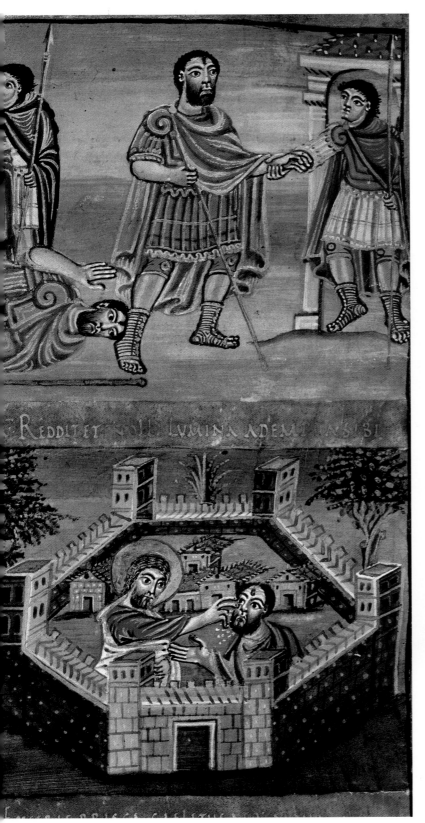

him leaving. Saul's friends, however, smuggled him out by lowering him in a basket through an opening in the city wall and he made his escape unobserved and hurried to Jerusalem.

The disciples were at first sceptical of Saul's conversion, but they were soon persuaded of his sincerity. Saul remained preaching in Jerusalem until threats to his life forced him to move to Tarsus. Then, with his companion Barnabas, he went to Antioch in Syria. They stayed there for a year, establishing a Christian following. Saul, now known as Paul, was finally ready to take the faith to the Gentiles of the Roman Empire.

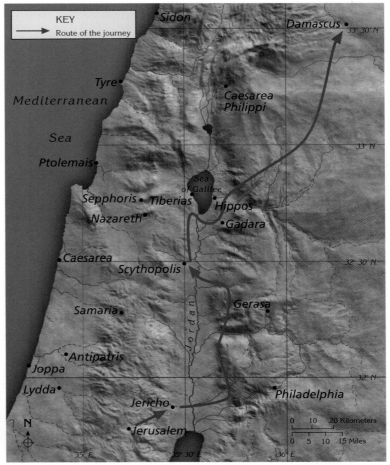

Saul's Journey to Damascus
The biblical account of Saul's journey from Jerusalem to Damascus lacks detail, but this map shows his most likely route and the towns through which he might have passed.

Saul was almost at the end of his journey when he was struck blind by a light from heaven. Once his sight was restored, Saul stayed in Damascus spreading the word of Jesus.

This 9th-century manuscript (above) depicts the story of Saul's conversion. In the top left-hand corner, Saul, on his way to Damascus, is blinded by a heavenly light. He is led to the house of Judas in Damascus where for three days he takes no food or water. Ananias is instructed by God in a dream to visit Saul (bottom left). Ananias blesses Saul (bottom right) and restores his sight.

The ancient city of Damascus that Saul would have known (right) was built on a grid pattern typical of Graeco-Roman design. This plan shows the two parallel main streets of the city. One ran between the agora (marketplace) and the Temple of Jupiter. The other, called Straight Street, ran past the theater and the former royal palace, the home of the Roman governor in Paul's day.

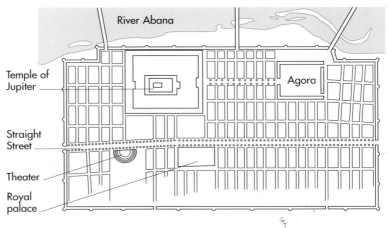

A manuscript portrait of St Paul

A man of fine intellect, indomitable spirit, and inexhaustible energy, Paul made three lengthy missionary journeys – as well as a final voyage as a prisoner to Rome – taking the Gospel into the heart of the Graeco-Roman world. Paul was able to argue the case for Christianity with Jews because he was a Jew himself. By the same token, he also had success preaching to Gentiles as he was born a Roman citizen and had grown up among people of many religions in the cosmopolitan city of Tarsus, in Asia Minor.

On all three missions, Paul traveled great distances by boat and on foot. The Mediterranean Sea had been swept clear of pirates in the previous century and provided relatively safe and easy access to most parts of the Empire. Once on land, Paul used the excellent Roman road network that linked the far-flung parts of the Empire together.

Paul's first journey took him from Antioch in Syria to Cyprus, and on to Pisidia in Asia Minor. He then headed east to Lystra – where he was stoned by a hostile crowd – and Derbe, before returning to Antioch.

On his second journey Paul entered Europe for the first time, preaching in the Greek cities of Thessalonica, Athens, and Corinth. His third journey featured a stay of more than two years in Ephesus in Asia Minor. Ephesus was one of the most important centers of worship of the pagan goddess Artemis, and Paul narrowly escaped being lynched by an angry mob during his time here.

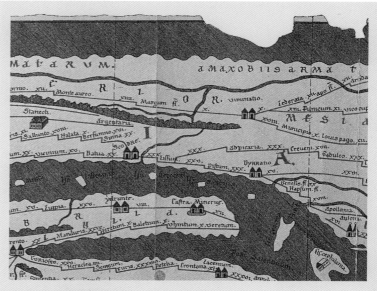

A Network of Roads
The well-known saying, 'All roads lead to Rome,' is graphically realized in the Peutinger map (above), a 13th-century copy of a late Roman original. The Roman network of paved roads was more than 88,500km (55,000 miles) long, and Paul traveled along several stretches of this network as he traversed the Empire preaching the Gospel.

From Ephesus, Paul traveled to Jerusalem, where he was arrested by the Roman authorities. His trial was transferred to Rome, where he continued to proclaim the Gospel until his death during the reign of the emperor Nero.

Paul's missions were a great success. He made numerous converts and probably did more than any other apostle to spread the new faith throughout the Roman Empire.

Paul would have entered Rome by the Via Appia, the main highway into the city from the south. The Via Appia demonstrates the best Roman roadbuilding techniques. The road surface was designed to drain quickly and so remain passable for a marching army in any weather.

The Romans were the undisputed masters of the Mediterranean world when Paul undertook his missionary journeys. Their technological skills enabled them to build the finest paved roads, capable of being used by a carriage drawn by galloping horses (below). But the Romans also enjoyed bloodthirsty sports, such as gladiatorial combat in which men fought to the death before large audiences. At the right is a perfectly preserved bronze helmet worn by one such gladiator.

Paul's Journeys
Between 46 and 54 CE, Paul made three long missionary journeys around the eastern Mediterranean. His final journey, probably begun in late 58 CE, took him to Rome for trial before the emperor.

KEY

→	Paul's 1st Journey
→	Paul's 2nd Journey
→	Paul's 3rd Journey – Stage 1
⋯	Paul's 3rd Journey – Stage 2
- -	Paul's 3rd Journey – Stage 3
→	Paul's 4th Journey

THRACIA
(THRACE)

GALATIA

MYSIA
Troas
Assos
Pergamum
Mitylene

PHRYGIA
Dorylaeum

Antioch in Pisidia
Iconium

CILICIA

Chios

PISIDIA
Lystra
Derbe
Tarsus

Antioch on the Orontes
Seleucia
SYRIA
Orontes

Ephesus
Miletus

Laodicea
Colossae
Attalia
Perge
LYCIA
PAMPHYLIA

Samos

Cos
Cnidus
Patara
Myra
Rhodes

CYPRUS

Salamis
Paphos

PHOENICIA
Sidon
Damascus
Tyre
Ptolemais

Salmone

CRETA
(Crete)
air-
Havens

Caesarea

JUDEA
Jerusalem

Dead
Sea

e a n   S e a

Sea

Alexandria

AEGYPTUS
(EGYPT)

0   50   100   150   200 Kilometers
0   50   100   150 Miles

Roman carving of a transport ship, typical of Paul's day

Paul's first missionary journey began in Antioch in Syria, where he and Barnabas, a convert from Cyprus, had been building up the local church. Under the guidance of the Holy Spirit, Paul, accompanied by Barnabas and John Mark, the likely author of the second Gospel, set sail for Cyprus.

Landing at Salamis, Paul and his companions made their way to Paphos in the southwest of the island. There they met Cyprus's Roman governor, Sergius Paulus, who showed an interest in their teachings. But Paul and Barnabas were obstructed in their efforts by Sergius' attendant, Bar-Jesus, a 'false prophet,' who probably feared he would fall from favor if the governor became a Christian. Paul, filled with the Holy Spirit, countered this by rebuking Bar-Jesus and causing him to become temporarily blind – an action that so impressed Sergius that he immediately became a believer.

Paul and his comrades then sailed to Perge, where John Mark left them to return to Jerusalem. Paul and Barnabas continued to Antioch in Pisidia where Paul preached to the

> ■ We bring you good news, that you should turn from these worthless things to the living God ...
>
> Acts 14:15

local Jewish community and to sympathetic Gentiles. Paul taught that God's promise of a Messiah had been fulfilled by Jesus, and that people's sins could be forgiven through Jesus, rather than through Jewish Law.

Paul is persecuted

Paul's sermon caused a great stir, but a number of Jews were angered by his teaching and tried to turn their people against him. In consequence, Paul decided to direct his message toward the Gentiles. Nevertheless, the Jews managed to convince some of Antioch's leading citizens that the two missionaries were trouble-makers and had them expelled.

Paul and Barnabas had a similar experience at their next port of call, Iconium in Galatia; fearing for their safety, they hurried south to Lystra. Here Paul healed a cripple, leading the local people to believe that he and Barnabas were the Greek gods Hermes and Zeus. Before they could teach any further, hostile Jews arrived from Antioch and Iconium and turned the Lystrans against them. Paul was stoned and left for dead. But he recovered, and escaped with Barnabas to Derbe, where they ended their mission. The two men then retraced their steps, strengthening the Christian communities they had founded in Lystra, Iconium, and Antioch in Pisidia.

Paul's First Journey
On his first journey and accompanied by the faithful Barnabas, Paul went from Syria to Cyprus, and then into Pisidia and Galatia, in what is now the modern state of Turkey. Paul and Barnabas had much success in spreading the word of Jesus, particularly among Gentiles, or non-Jews. However, their teaching that anyone could find salvation through Jesus angered many Jews, who threatened their lives on more than one occasion.

Salamis, in Cyprus, *was Paul's first port of call after leaving Syria. Salamis was a Roman town at the time and contained a splendid amphitheater (on the left in this aerial photograph) and a gymnasium (on the right). Paul and his companions crossed Cyprus to Paphos in the southwest, where they converted the Roman governor, Sergius Paulus.*

Gods of the Lystrans

When Paul visited Lystra he healed a cripple, leading the people to believe that he and Barnabas were the Greek gods Hermes and Zeus. The Lystrans began to organize a sacrifice in their honor, forcing Paul and Barnabas to deny strongly that they were gods at all. Instead, they explained that they bore news about the one true God. The Greek deities were very different in concept from the Christian God. To begin with there were many of them, both gods and goddesses, led by Zeus (shown left), ruler of the gods. Barnabas must have greatly impressed the Lystrans for them to link him with this powerful figure. Paul was thought to be Hermes (shown right), the son of Zeus and messenger of the gods. Hermes was also associated with medicine, explaining, perhaps, why Paul was identified with him after he healed a cripple. Both of these Greek gods had great powers, but they were also fallible and prey to all the usual human desires and weaknesses. Unlike the Christian God, these deities had nothing to offer humans in the way of salvation.

*A **watchtower** in the ruined city wall of Perge (above). Paul arrived in Perge from Cyprus in about 47 CE, and it was here that he gave his first sermon in Asia Minor. John Mark, who had accompanied Paul and Barnabas from Antioch in Syria, left his companions here to return to Jerusalem.*

Monument beside the Via Egnatia in Macedonia

Paul successfully established several Christian centers on his first missionary journey to Asia Minor. Anxious that these should not be neglected, he decided to set out with a disciple named Silas to revisit them. They left from Antioch in Syria and traveled westward overland to Derbe, Lystra, Iconium, and Antioch in Pisidia, being joined at Lystra by Timothy, a new convert.

Guided by the Holy Spirit, they then continued across Phrygia to Troas on the Aegean. Here Paul had a vision of a Macedonian man begging him to come to his people. Paul responded at once and the party set sail across the Aegean to Macedonia.

The mission in Greece

First they landed in the Roman colony of Philippi, where after speaking to a gathering of women, Paul baptized 'a worshiper of God,' Lydia, and her household. Here too he exorcised a slave-girl of an evil spirit that had enabled her to tell fortunes. This infuriated the girl's owners, who saw they could no longer earn money from her. They had Paul and Silas flogged and jailed. That night, an earthquake loosened the prisoners' chains, astonishing their jailer who immediately became a convert. Then they were released and escorted from the city.

Taking the Via Egnatia, the Roman road that crossed Macedonia, the missionaries came to Thessalonica. Paul's

■ ...Paul had a vision: there stood a man of Macedonia pleading with him and saying, 'Come over to Macedonia and help us.'

Acts 16:9

initial success here was countered by some fierce Jewish opposition, so they moved on. At Beroea, Paul found a receptive audience, but the arrival of hostile Jews from Thessalonica once again forced his departure.

Paul then continued alone to Athens. In Athens, the great intellectual center of the ancient world, he entered into an animated debate with a group of philosophers on the Areopagus Hill. But when he mentioned Jesus' resurrection he was greeted with derision. Distressed by this response and having made only a handful of converts, Paul left for Corinth.

Silas and Timothy rejoined him there and Paul preached in the Corinth synagogue until Jewish hostility drove him away. Undeterred, he stayed in Corinth for over a year, preaching particularly to the Gentiles before returning to Antioch via Ephesus, Caesarea, and Jerusalem. Although Paul was initially disheartened by his experiences in Macedonia, his work there established several Christian centers, and attracted many converts, especially among Gentiles.

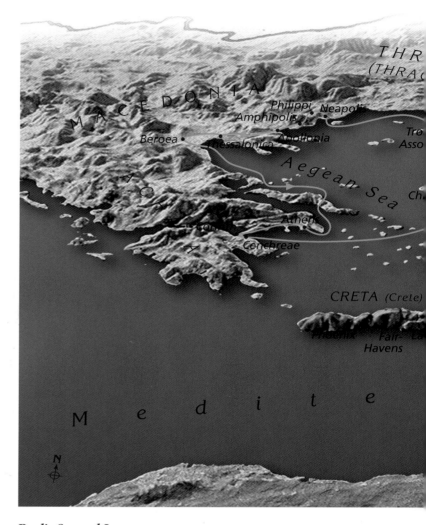

Paul's Second Journey
Paul's original purpose in embarking on his second missionary journey was to strengthen the churches he had established on his first. He began by retracing his steps, only venturing across the Aegean into Europe in response to a vision from God. Although he faced severe, sometimes violent, opposition from Jewish communities in Macedonia, Paul succeeded in introducing Christianity to all the cities he visited. His return journey, by sea from Corinth, included a stop at Ephesus, which he also revisited on his third journey. Brief stops at Caesarea and Jerusalem completed his route.

Antioch in Pisidia, with its impressive Roman aqueduct, had come under Roman control in 25 BCE. It was probably Paul's last port of call in familiar territory before he branched northwestward across Phrygia to the Aegean.

Philippi, a Roman colony, now reduced to ruins, was Paul's first destination in Macedonia. Despite being Roman citizens, he and Silas were flogged and thrown into jail here on trumped up charges of troublemaking.

Corinth, whose Temple of Apollo (left) dominated the city, was one of the great trading centers of ancient Greece, and it retained its importance into Roman times. The unfriendly reception that Paul received from the Jews in Corinth led him to concentrate on addressing his message to the Gentiles instead. This policy met with such success that Paul stayed on for over a year and was able to establish a flourishing Christian church. He found converts even among the higher echelons of Corinth society. In his Letter to the Romans, *Paul* mentions that Corinth's 'director of public works' was a convert. This marble pavingblock at Corinth (below) is inscribed with the name 'Erastus Proaedilis', who is believed to have been that same director of public works.

The Areopagus (above) in Athens is approached now, as in Paul's time, by stone steps. It is a low prominence near the Acropolis where in ancient times a council of learned men gathered to discuss and judge new ideas. Paul was brought here to hold a formal debate with a group of philosophers. Paul's arguments met with little success once he mentioned Jesus' resurrection, an idea that the Greeks derided. Paul must have been disappointed in Athens since he left it at the earliest opportunity, although he did make a few converts in the short time he was there.

Patara, where Paul changed ships on his way home

Paul's third mission to spread the word of Jesus took him back to Ephesus in Asia Minor, a major trading city and center of worship of the goddess Artemis or Diana.

Paul had visited Ephesus briefly on his second journey and had promised to return. He traveled from Antioch by way of Galatia and Phrygia, visiting some of the churches founded on his previous journeys. Paul taught for three months in the local synagogue at Ephesus until he was forced out by hostile Jews, who were disturbed by his teachings and his involvement in various spiritual events. On one occasion, for instance, Paul rebaptized in Jesus' name 12 Christians previously baptized by John the Baptist. Immediately they were filled with the Holy Spirit and began to speak in tongues. Later he met a group of seven Jewish exorcists who tried, in the name of Jesus, to cast an evil spirit out of a possessed man. The spirit refused and amazed them by saying that he recognized the authority of Jesus and Paul, but not that of Jewish exorcists. With such happenings associated with him, Paul's reputation spread.

Paul leaves Ephesus

Paul's fame did not come without risk. Local silversmiths, under their leader Demetrius, became angered by Paul's

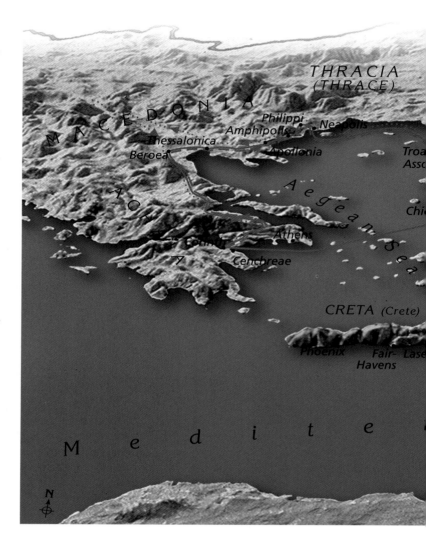

■ 'Not only in Ephesus but in almost the whole of Asia this Paul has persuaded and drawn away a considerable number of people ...'

Acts 19:26

stance against idols, which was affecting their trade in effigies for the Temple of Artemis. They incited a mob to drag two of Paul's men to the city's theater, aiming to have them tried. Paul was restrained from intervening by friends concerned for his safety. After a tense two hours, the city clerk managed to calm the situation by threatening that the city would be in trouble if news of the rioting reached the Roman authorities.

After this, Paul hurriedly left Ephesus for Macedonia and Greece. He rejoined some of his followers in Troas, where he revived a boy who had been killed in a fall from an upstairs window. Paul then began his voyage home, meeting the leaders of the Ephesian church for a final farewell at Miletus.

After changing ships at Patara, Paul landed at Tyre and traveled on to Ptolemais and Caesarea. In Tyre the Holy Spirit warned that Paul should not go to Jerusalem, and at Caesarea, Agabus, a prophet, foretold that Paul's Jewish enemies in Jerusalem would hand him over to the Romans. But Paul ignored these portents, preparing for the journey to David's city saying that he was ready to die in Jesus' name.

Paul's Third Journey
Paul probably reached Ephesus in the summer of 52 CE and stayed there for over two years. During this time he may also have sailed to Corinth to sort out problems in the church there. He finally left Ephesus after the silversmiths' riot and headed back to Achaia via Macedonia and possibly Illiricum to the northwest. His journey home took him overland to Troas and then by boat back to Tyre.

The Taurus Mountains *lie to the north and west of Tarsus, Paul's birthplace and the chief city in the Roman province of Cilicia. The only good trade route between Asia Minor and Syria passed through a narrow gorge in the mountains known as the Cilician Gates. This is the route Paul took during both his second and third journeys as he traveled west toward the city of Ephesus.*

KEY
→ Paul's 3rd journey – stage 1
•••→ Paul's 3rd journey – stage 2
– –→ Paul's 3rd journey – stage 3

GALATIA

MYSIA

PHRYGIA

Dorylaeum

Antioch in Pisidia

Iconium

CILICIA

Pergamum

Mitylene

PISIDIA

Lystra

Derbe

Antioch on
the Orontes

Laodicea

Colossae

PAMPHYLIA

Seleucia

Ephesus

LYCIA

Attalia

Perge

SYRIA

Miletus

Orontes

Cos

Cnidus

Patara

Myra

CYPRUS

Salamis

PHOENICIA

Damascus

Rhodes

Paphos

Salmone

Sidon
Tyre
Ptolemais

Caesarea

Jordan

Mediterranean Sea

JUDEA

Jerusalem

Dead
Sea

Alexandria

AEGYPTUS
(EGYPT)

0   50   100   150   200 Kilometers
0   50   100   150 Miles

N

Assos in Asia Minor was a major seaport in Paul's day. It lies a little to the south of Troas, and its harbor wall (above) dates back to ancient times. Paul stopped at Troas on the return leg of his third journey and preached to a gathering in an upstairs room. He went on for so long that a youth fell asleep, toppled out of the window and was killed. By a miracle, however, Paul was able to revive him. Paul then traveled overland to Assos, where he met up with his companions and continued his journey by ship to Mitylene and Miletus, before crossing the eastern Mediterranean to Tyre.

The port of Tyre in Phoenicia is rich in Roman remains, such as the hippodrome, or racetrack (above). Paul visited Tyre at the end of his third journey, staying here with his disciples for a week. While he was there, the Holy Spirit warned the disciples of great danger facing Paul in Jerusalem so they urged him not to go there. Before leaving Tyre, Paul led the Christian community out of the city to the beach, where they knelt and prayed with him. Then they bid him farewell as he boarded a ship bound for Ptolemais. From there, Paul went to Caesarea and then, despite the warnings, carried on to Jerusalem.

The city of Ephesus was the main center of Paul's teaching for over two years of his third journey. The city stood at the mouth of the River Cayster on the Aegean coast of Asia Minor and was originally settled by Mycenean immigrants before 1200 BCE. Ephesus grew in size and prosperity to become one of the greatest cities of the Roman Empire, with a population at its height of over a quarter of a million.

One reason for Ephesus' importance was economic: with its sheltered harbor, the city became a major center for trade between Asia Minor and the rest of Rome's Mediterranean empire. Another reason was cultural: the city's population was drawn from many parts of the Empire and it boasted a very impressive array of civic amenities, including a theater that seated over 24,000 spectators. Other public buildings included a town hall and library, two marketplaces, baths, fountains, gymnasia, and a stadium.

The many-breasted Artemis of Ephesus

the city, bringing in much wealth. The temple and cult of Artemis supported many local trades and industries, such as the manufacture and sale of votive images of the goddess. The owners of such enterprises were particularly opposed to Paul's Christian teaching, since anything that undermined the cult of Artemis also threatened their commercial interests.

Perhaps the concentration of religious cults and occult interests in Ephesus also made many of its citizens predisposed to listen to the new Christian message. Certainly Paul's efforts firmly established the new religion in this most pagan of cities. Ephesus ultimately became the most important center of Christianity in the whole of Roman Asia Minor, and a remained a vibrant city as late as the 5th century.

But Ephesus' days of prosperity were numbered. The harbor began to silt up, reducing seaborne trade. The economy and population declined steadily from the late Roman period, and today Ephesus lies in ruins.

> ■ '...the city of the Ephesians is the temple keeper of the great Artemis and of the statue that fell from heaven...'
>
> Acts 19:35

Artemis of the Ephesians

Ephesus also had a great religious significance: it was the center of a major cult of the goddess Artemis, or Diana. The Artemis of Ephesus had taken on many attributes of the ancient Near Eastern Mother Goddess, and her temple, built around 335 BCE, was one of the Seven Wonders of the World.

Ephesus was also a center for practitioners of the occult, including fortune-tellers and astrologers. Pilgrims flocked to

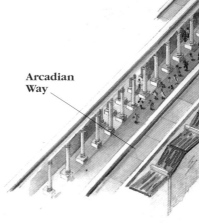

Ephesus in Paul's day
Paul's two-year stay in Ephesus coincided with a period of great changes in the city. The old town, based around the temple of Artemis, had been abandoned some 300 years earlier, and construction in the new city was in full flow by the time Paul arrived. The temple lay some distance to the northeast of the new city, and is therefore not shown here. Work went on for many years; the theater, for instance, took well over 70 years to complete.

Arcadian Way

To the harbour

This footprint, *cut into a marble pavement in Ephesus, indicated the entrance to a brothel. The cosmopolitan cities of Asia Minor were well known for their immorality and their conspicuous displays of wealth, perhaps making Paul's message of forgiveness and salvation all the more appealing to them.*

The theater *was the focus of the city and stood at the top of the Arcadian Way. The original theater dated from the 3rd century BCE and was enlarged in Roman times. It was to here that a mob, angered at Paul's criticism of idol worship and led by the silversmiths, dragged Paul's companions for trial.*

The House *of the Virgin Mary outside Ephesus owes its name to an ancient legend that Mary was brought to the city by St John after Jesus' crucifixion and lived out her last years there. Tradition also says that John himself lived in Ephesus in his old age and that it was here that he wrote his Gospel.*

The Arcadian Way (right) *led from the harbor directly to the theater, the focal point of the new city. This ceremonial road was paved in marble and colonnaded on both sides. Originally laid out in the 1st century BCE, it was later rebuilt and even included street lighting along its entire length.*

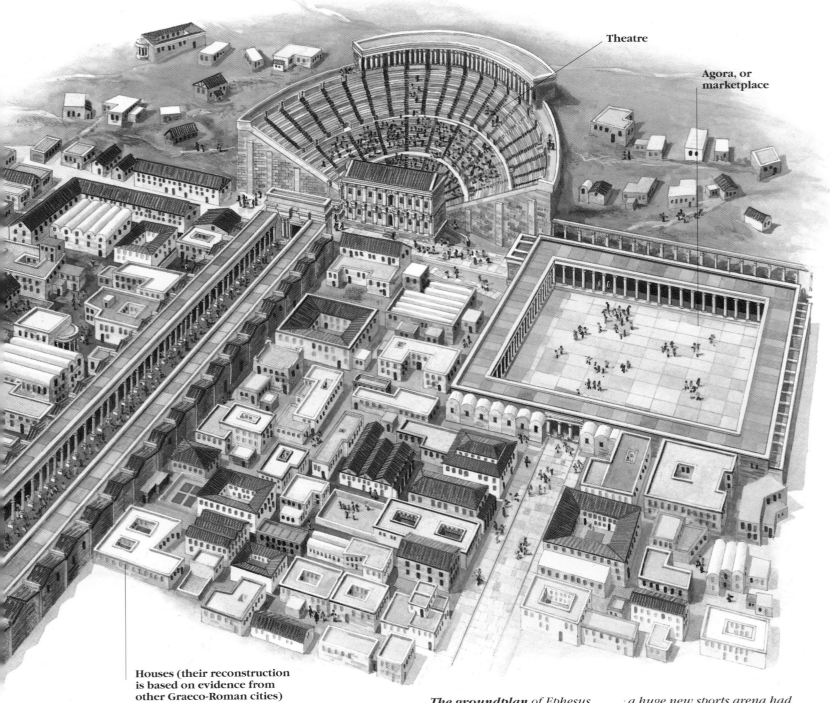

Theatre

Agora, or marketplace

Houses (their reconstruction
is based on evidence from
other Graeco-Roman cities)

The groundplan of Ephesus
below shows the city in the
2nd century CE, by which time
it had grown considerably
since Paul's visits. For example,
a huge new sports arena had
been built close to the theater.
Shading indicates features or
buildings that also appear in
the above reconstruction.

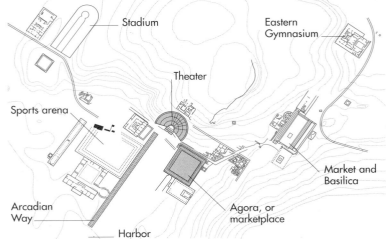

Stadium

Eastern
Gymnasium

Theater

Sports arena

Market and
Basilica

Arcadian
Way

Agora, or
marketplace

Harbor

Coin bearing a portrait of Herod Agrippa II

Back in Jerusalem after his third missionary journey, Paul was welcomed by the church elders. However, on a visit to the Temple he was unjustly accused by some Jews of bringing Gentiles into a prohibited area. In the resultant uproar, a mob attacked Paul and tried to kill him. On hearing the commotion, the city's Roman commander had Paul arrested. He was also about to have him flogged and interrogated when he learned that Paul was a Roman citizen, and therefore legally immune from punishment without trial. He then asked the Sanhedrin, the Jewish council, to clarify exactly what Paul had done wrong. Confronting the Sanhedrin elders, Paul deliberately set off a fierce argument between the council's two main parties, the

> ■ I have in no way committed an offense against the law of the Jews, or against the temple, or against the emperor.
>
> Acts 25:8

Sadducees and Pharisees, and the Roman commander was again forced to arrest Paul for his own safety.

That night, in a vision, God told Paul that just as he had testified about God in Jerusalem, so he would have to testify in Rome. The next day, the commander heard of a Jewish plot to kill Paul and so sent him under armed guard to Caesarea, headquarters of Antonius Felix, the Roman governor of Judea. Felix heard Paul's case after his accusers arrived with Tertullus, a lawyer. Paul vehemently denied charges that he had stirred up riots or desecrated the Temple. He said that he believed in the Jewish Law but was also a follower of 'the Way' – meaning Jesus' teachings. He had come to Jerusalem, he said, to bring money to the Christian poor, and he denied any wrongdoing. He ended by challenging his accusers to state what crime he had committed; but they could not.

Paul demands trial in Rome

Impressed by Paul's words, Felix adjourned the case but kept Paul under house arrest for two years, perhaps hoping that Paul would offer him a bribe. When a new governor, Porcius Festus, was appointed, the Jewish authorities renewed their charges against Paul, but still they were unable to prove them. Paul maintained his innocence and then asserted his right as a Roman citizen to face trial in Rome before the emperor.

Paul was also interviewed by Herod Agrippa II, a local king, and his sister Bernice. Paul spoke of his life and his mission to tell both Jews and Gentiles about Jesus. His words persuaded Agrippa that he was innocent of any crime, and he and the Roman authorities agreed that Paul could have been set free had he not demanded to be tried before the emperor.

The Antonia Fortress *was the headquarters of the Roman guard and Paul was probably imprisoned here after his arrest by the Romans. The fortress had been rebuilt by Herod the Great on the site of an earlier fort just outside the northwest corner of the Temple. Herod named it after his ally, Mark Antony. Nothing is left of the original building; the reconstruction shown here is part of a scale model in Jerusalem of the entire Temple complex.*

Roman soldiers, *such as these shown in a Roman mosaic, were stationed throughout Judea. Their presence was deeply resented, but they were crucial in keeping the peace in the province. When attacked by a mob at the Temple, Paul owed his life to the Roman soldiers who arrested him on the orders of their commander.*

The Court of the Gentiles was the only area of the Temple at Jerusalem which non-Jews could enter. Warning notices carved in several languages on stone slabs prohibited entry to the inner courts. Still visible on this fragment of one of the slabs (right) is part of the inscription in Greek: 'No Gentile may enter beyond the dividing wall into the court around the holy place; whoever is caught will be to blame for his subsequent death.'

Caesarea, headquarters of the Roman provincial governor of Judea, had been built by Herod the Great in Roman style with many imposing features, including its aqueduct (above). Paul was taken to Caesarea under armed guard to be examined by the governor Antonius Felix.

Roman Citizenship

In its early days, Rome regarded only its free-born inhabitants as citizens. As its borders extended ever further, Rome granted citizenship to individuals who were not of Roman birth, such as soldiers recruited in the provinces, and to the members of whole communities to reward them for their services or to gain their loyalty. New citizens were given a certificate of Roman citizenship (*diploma civitatis Romanae*) bearing their new Roman names which could be used as proof of identity throughout the Roman Empire. A similar certificate would often be carried by someone born a Roman citizen, like Paul, whose Roman name 'Paulus' was probably chosen because of its similarity to Saul. A citizen was entitled to legal protection, including the right to appeal against a sentence to the emperor himself at Rome. Roman tradesmen, like the metalworkers depicted in the 1st-century stone relief from Pompeii above, could seek a magistrate's help to enforce a commercial contract.

Aerial view of the reconstructed remains of Caesarea's theatre

Built by Herod the Great between 22 and 10 BCE, the city of Caesarea became the Roman seat of power in Judea. It was named after the Roman emperor Augustus Caesar, and features prominently in the New Testament. Paul passed through Caesarea several times and was kept there under house arrest for two years by governor Felix, before being sent to Rome for trial.

Herod, the Roman-appointed king of Judea, constructed the city on the site of a 3rd-century BCE Phoenician settlement named Strato's Tower. This had fallen into the hands of the Roman general Pompey in 63 BCE. Octavian – the future Emperor Augustus – granted it to Herod in 30 BCE and he set about rebuilding it on a grand scale. The city's most impressive structure was its artificial harbor, whose two sturdy breakwaters sheltered shipping and, to a large extent, prevented the harbor from silting up. The port brought commerce to the city, which became a major center for purple-dyeing – a complex and lucrative process at that time.

Herod beautified the city with several fine civic and religious buildings. A temple dedicated to Augustus overlooked the harbor, while a huge oval amphitheater dominated the sea front, and a grand palace sat high up on a promontory. To the north, an aqueduct carried water from springs at Mount Carmel, 21 kilometers (13 miles) away.

Herod wanted Caesarea to remain Graeco-Syrian in character, but the Jewish population of the city demanded to have the same civic rights as their Gentile neighbors. This created tensions and in about 60 CE rioting broke out. Jewish grievances were dismissed by Emperor Nero and, in 66 CE, more rioting led to a massacre of Jews. This was one of the sparks that ignited the great Jewish rebellion against Rome. Meanwhile, Caesarea became the headquarters of commander Vespasian, who was proclaimed Emperor of Rome in 69 CE, while residing in the city.

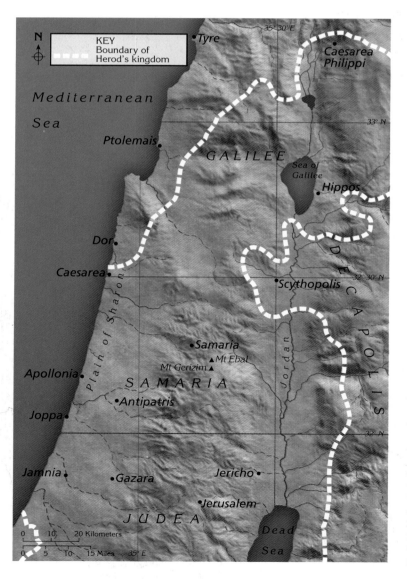

Lighthouse

Breakwater

Breakwater

Outer harbor

The Port of Caesarea
Caesarea was situated on the Mediterranean coast, midway between the seaports of Ptolemais and Joppa. Herod the Great spent 12 years building his splendid new city port, which was also to serve as his administrative headquarters outside Jerusalem. The city, with its imposing artificial harbor, later became the Roman capital of Judea. This map shows the location of Caesarea in relation to other major towns of the region.

Herod's Caesarea
The maritime city of Caesarea was one of the grandest schemes in Herod the Great's prolific building program. In naming the kingdom's first true seaport 'Caesarea,' Herod also managed to flatter his Roman patron, Augustus Caesar. The city was a model settlement. Built on a grid street plan, it had lavish buildings and an ingenious sewerage network beneath its streets which was flushed out by sea tides and currents.

Recent excavations *at Caesarea have uncovered the remains of an amphitheater which had been buried for centuries beneath layers of marine sediments. Although it is shaped like a hippodrome (or racetrack), the Jewish historian Josephus described the structure that lay 'along the shore' as an amphitheater.*

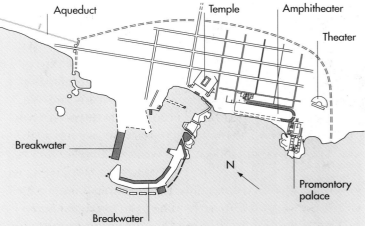

The plan of Caesarea *above shows the port during Herod's time. The most impressive structure was the artificial harbor, which was dominated by the large, pincer-shaped breakwaters. The city was enclosed on the landward side by a semicircular perimeter wall. The neat grid system adopted for the streets can also be seen.*

Aqueduct

Inner harbor

Temple

Agora

Streets laid out on a grid pattern

Perimeter wall

Amphitheater

Promontory palace

Theater

Paul's Letters

Of the 21 epistles, or letters, in the New Testament, at least seven are undisputedly by Paul and a further six are ascribed to him. Some of these letters may have been written as early as 50 CE, making them the first known Christian texts, perhaps preceding Mark's Gospel by ten years.

As a cosmopolitan Jew, Paul wrote in Greek – the language of learning in the eastern Roman Empire. Some of his letters were written during his imprisonments in Caesarea and Rome, others come from his years on the road. His second letter to the Corinthians, for instance was written on his third journey, probably at Philippi.

Paul generally dictated his letters to a secretary, sometimes adding a postscript of his own. The letters would have been written on papyrus – made by cutting

the stems of papyrus plants into thin strips and beating them into flat sheets. Although the Romans had an efficient postal service, it was reserved for official business; private individuals such as Paul had to arrange with friends or traders to deliver correspondence.

Many of Paul's letters deal with problems specific to certain churches. Writing to the Corinthians, for example, Paul deals with sexual relationships, and to the Galatians he sends assurances that circumcision is irrelevant to Gentile Christians, emphasizing that faith through love is far more important. In his epistle to the Ephesians, Paul drew parallels between Christ's love for his church and proper relationships within families.

In other places Paul's letters discuss issues of theology affecting the Church as a whole. For example, when writing to believers in Rome and Ephesus, he explored the idea of the redemptive power of Christ's sacrificial death, explaining how people can be saved from their sins by faith in God alone. Like many of Paul's ideas, this was immensely influential on the emerging Church.

Above: Greek text of the *Codex Sinaiticus*, the oldest known complete New Testament manuscript. **Background:** The Forum and the Via Sacra in Rome. **Map:** Some sites visited by Paul.

1. Caesarea, where Paul was detained for two years.
2. 'St Paul's Prison' at Philippi where Paul may have been held.
3. Papyrus plants.
4. Roman ink pot.

Corinth
Aegean Sea
Athens Ephesus

Rhodes

0   10 Kilometers
0   4   8 Miles

③

④

Paul, on the left, appears before Emperor Nero, seated right

Paul was kept under house arrest by the Roman governor for two years before being finally sent to Rome to stand trial before the emperor. He left with a group of prisoners, possibly accompanied by Luke the Gospel writer. They began their journey from Caesarea by ship calling at several ports along the way. By the time they arrived in Myra on the south coast of Asia Minor, it was late in the year and bad weather threatened. Even so, they were transferred to a cargo ship and sent off to Rome.

Shipwreck on Malta

As they proceeded westward the weather worsened. South of Crete, they ran into a severe storm and tried to run for shelter to the port of Phoenix. Both passengers and crew feared for their lives, but Paul comforted them by relating a vision he had the night before in which an angel assured him that he would appear before the emperor and that God would protect them. For the next fortnight, the ship was lashed by strong winds and high seas. Finally, they neared land – the island of Malta – but the ship struck a sandbar and started to break up. The soldiers wanted to kill the prisoners to ensure that none escaped, but in the event all made it safely to shore. Here they were received kindly, and Paul cured the ailing father of the Roman governor of Malta, as well as others who came to him to be healed.

Paul in Rome

After three months on Malta, Paul and his companions were put on to another cargo ship to continue their journey. They disembarked at Puteoli near Naples, where Paul spent a week as the guest of some Christians there, before traveling on to Rome by land. As Paul entered the city he was greeted by a deputation of Roman Christians.

The authorities placed Paul under house arrest, but allowed him to write and to receive visitors and preach. The Bible says that Paul spent two years in Rome, but the account ends abruptly, without stating whether or not he stood trial. One early Christian tradition says that Paul went on to spread

> ■ Since the ship was caught and could not be turned head-on into the wind, we gave way to it and were driven.
>
> Acts 27:15

Paul's route to Rome

Paul's final journey to Rome is described in detail in the Acts of the Apostles. Three ships were involved: first a coaster which called at various ports between Caesarea and Myra; then a grain ship on its way from Egypt to Rome, which was wrecked off Malta; and finally another grain ship which had sheltered through the winter on Malta. Paul landed at Puteoli near Naples and continued his journey to Rome on foot.

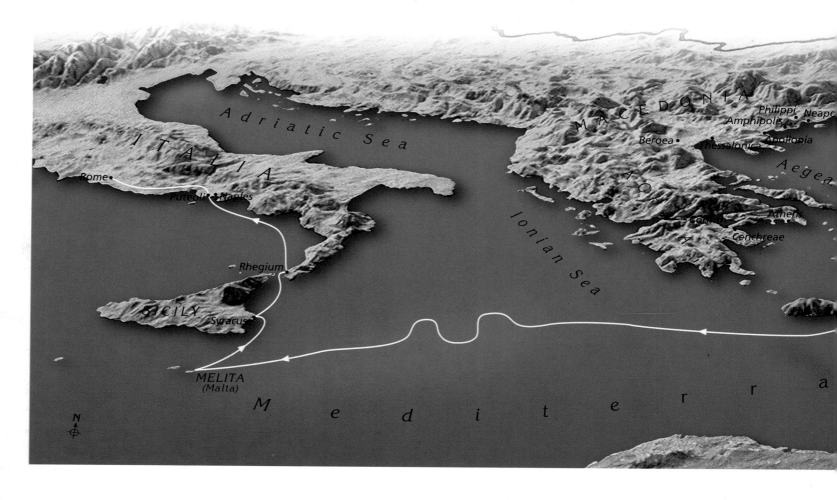

St Paul's Bay is traditionally said to be the place where Paul and his shipmates struggled ashore on Malta following their shipwreck. Beyond the bay is a sandy spit which corresponds well with the description of the sandbar given in the Bible.

Myra was one of the chief cities of the Roman province of Lycia, and Paul's first stop on his journey to Rome. The area is rich in remains from the Roman period and earlier, such as the tombs from the 4th century BCE pictured above.

the Gospel in Spain before returning to Rome. But most scholars believe that he died in Rome, perhaps during Nero's persecution of the Christians in 64 CE. As a Roman citizen, if he had been executed, he would have been spared the agony of crucifixion in favor of beheading.

What the Bible does make clear is that the word of God had now reached the center of the known world. Jesus had predicted the spread of the Gospel to the 'ends of the earth;' and in helping to achieve this Paul had brought Christianity to the greatest city of the West, Rome. From its beginnings there, Christianity would become the faith of the entire Empire.

Puteoli

Paul landed at Puteoli (modern Pozzuoli) west of Naples, on the final stage of his eventful sea journey from Caesarea. He then traveled overland to Rome. The ancient harbor at Puteoli, pictured above in a painting from nearby Pompeii, was the main port of call for the great cargo ships that brought grain from Alexandria in Egypt to Rome. Since Roman times the land has subsided, but remains of the old harbor can still be seen under the waters of the Bay of Naples.

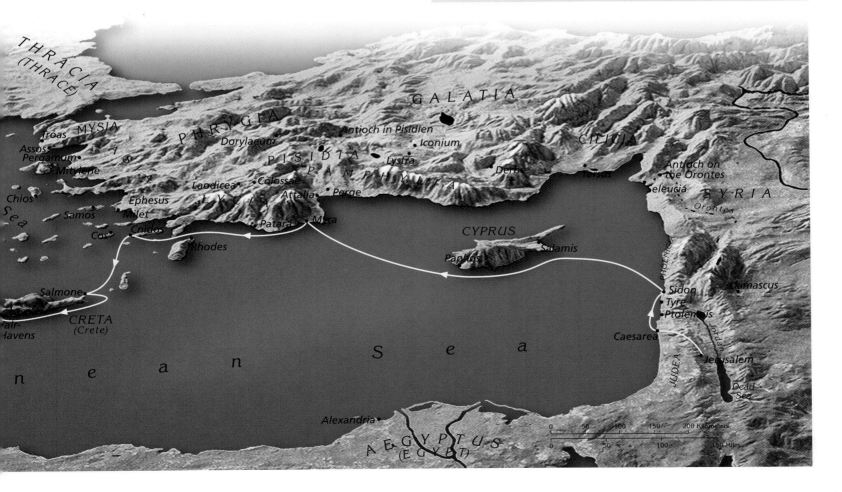

Marble head of Titus, Roman victor over the Jewish rebels

In 66 CE, after years of unrest, the Jews finally rose up against their Roman overlords. But their rebellion was defeated, and it resulted in the death and enslavement of thousands of Jews and the dispersion abroad of a great many others. Jerusalem was sacked and the Temple, recently enlarged and embellished by Herod the Great, was destroyed, never to rise again. The last vestiges of Jewish rule in the Holy Land were swept away, until the establishment of modern Israel in 1948.

The revolt was the culmination of years of increasing friction between Jews and the Roman authorities, made worse by a succession of inefficient, corrupt, and insensitive Roman procurators, or governors. Many Jews had never been able to reconcile themselves to Roman rule: they considered it insufferable that they – God's chosen people – should have to pay taxes to a pagan emperor. As early as 6 CE, the year the Romans assumed direct rule over Judea, a nationalist named Judas had led an abortive uprising. Over the following years Jewish freedom fighters, known as Zealots, continued to cause sporadic trouble. Discontent was particularly widespread during the time of Pontius Pilate (26–36 CE); and Emperor Caligula nearly caused a revolt in 39–40 CE by ordering a statue of himself to be erected in the Temple.

The great rebellion

According to the historian Josephus, who fought in the rebellion of 66–70 CE, the governorship of Antonius Felix (52–60 CE) was marked by increasing unrest in Judea, and the appearance of Jewish miracle workers promising deliverance from their oppressors. Then, in 66 CE, the last procurator, Gessius Florus, demanded gold from the Temple treasury, causing hundreds of Jews to protest on the streets. Florus sent in his troops to halt these disturbances, and in the conflicts that followed more than 3500 Jews were killed.

Florus' actions led to open revolt. Roman garrisons in Jerusalem and elsewhere were attacked and in response Cestius Gallus, the governor of Syria, advanced on Jerusalem with the Twelfth Legion to regain control. With the onset of winter, however, he retreated from the city and his army was ambushed and decimated by rebel forces at Beth-horon. Then, despite divisions between the rebel groups, the Jews set up an organized military command and prepared their defenses.

In response, Emperor Nero sent a seasoned campaigner named Vespasian to quash the rebellion with a powerful force of three legions (about 60,000 men). Vespasian opened his campaign in 67 CE by systematically overrunning Galilee, capturing its Jewish commander, Josephus. In the meantime, factional fighting broke out among the rebels in Judea.

Roman Siege Tactics

The Romans raised siege warfare to a fine art. They began by surrounding an enemy position with a rampart and palisade to ensure the defenders could not escape. If the enemy refused to surrender, a range of devices was used to break down their defenses. Among these were catapults that threw stones or shot heavy metal arrows; scaling ladders; and mobile siege towers with battering rams and drawbridges. When units advanced against the enemy walls, they used the 'tortoise' formation, with shields held above them to protect them from missiles. Few enemy strongholds were able to resist such tactics.

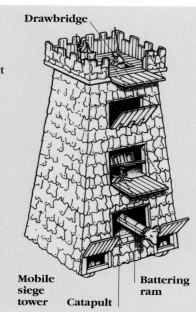

Drawbridge

Mobile siege tower   Catapult   Battering ram

The Arch of Titus, *built at the eastern end of the Forum in Rome in 81 CE, commemorates Titus' campaign against the Jewish rebels. The detail above, part of the left-hand inner relief panel, shows Roman soldiers in the triumphal procession following Titus' sack of Jerusalem. They are carrying treasures taken from the city, including the great menorah (seven-branched candelabrum) that stood in the Temple.*

Vespasian then advanced against Judea, defeating a group of Samaritan rebels on the way and securing the coastal cities of Jamnia and Azotus (Ashdod) to protect his lines of supply. In 68 CE, he cleared the Jordan Valley and the country around Emmaus, isolating Jerusalem. The next year Nero died, and Vespasian became emperor. He returned to Rome, leaving his son Titus to carry on operations in Judea. Titus immediately laid siege to Jerusalem with an army of four legions.

Despite its strong position and powerful defenses, Jerusalem fell after a five-month siege. The defenders were weakened first by factional fighting within the city and then by starvation – Josephus reports that some even turned to cannibalism. On about 28 August 70 CE, having breached the walls, Roman troops stormed the Temple; Jewish resistance in the city finally ended in late September. Both the Temple and the city were looted and razed. Yet, even though Jerusalem had fallen, there remained pockets of resistance, notably at the Zealot stronghold of Masada by the Dead Sea.

The Jewish Revolt
The revolt of the Jews against Roman rule in 67 CE spread quickly from Jerusalem and other cities. But Samaritan support for the rebels was limited, and the overall effort was weakened when fighting broke out between rival rebel groups, most notably between the Zealots and the Jewish aristocracy. By 69 CE the Romans had retaken the whole province apart from the large area bounded by Jerusalem, Herodium, Masada, and Machaerus. Titus' four legions converged on Jerusalem, the Jewish capital, in May 70 CE.

A Roman coin (right) dating from the time of Titus. Around the edge is the inscription 'Iudaea capta' (Judea captured). The issue of such coins, and the building of the Arch of Titus in the Forum, show clearly that the Romans regarded the suppression of the Jewish rebellion as a major military achievement. The campaign lasted over four years and involved a series of hard-fought sieges.

Coin minted for Simon Bar-Kokhba

Jewish resistance to Roman rule did not end with the destruction of Jerusalem in 70 CE. The last chapter in this struggle took place at Masada, a great rock rising up above the western shore of the Dead Sea. In this isolated and imposing location, Herod the Great had built himself a magnificent palace-fortress, equipping it with strong defenses and large cisterns for storing water in times of siege.

After Herod's death in 4 BCE, Masada passed into Roman hands. Then, in 66 CE, a determined force of Zealots – Jewish independence fighters – overcame the Roman garrison and set up a base there from which to conduct guerilla operations. In 73 CE the Roman governor Flavius Silva decided to put an end to the resistance once and for all. Advancing on Masada with the 10th Legion – a force of about 6000 regulars supplemented by about 4500 auxiliaries – Silva set up camp and prepared to lay siege. He began by building a huge ramp of earth and rubble to reach the walls at the top of the cliff, and then pounded the defenses with a battering ram. A breach was made, but the defenders hastily built an inner wall of earth and wood to fill it. Flavius ordered his troops to set fire to this new obstacle. At first the fire was blown back in their faces, but suddenly the wind changed direction and the flames engulfed the defenders' last barrier.

The last hours of the rebels

Meanwhile, within the fortress, the defenders realized that defeat was now just a matter of time. Their leader, Eleazar ben Yair, persuaded his people that it would be better to die than be taken alive. In one of the grimmest and most courageous episodes in Jewish history, the men began by killing the women and children – each man being responsible for his own family. Then ten men were chosen by lot to kill the others. Finally one man was singled out to kill the other nine and then he turned his sword upon himself.

When the Romans eventually broke in, prepared for a last ferocious bout of fighting, they were met by an eerie silence and the corpses of the defenders – 960 men, women, and children. There were only seven survivors: two women – one a relative of Eleazar – and five children who had hidden in an underground cavern while the mass suicide was taking place. When they emerged to tell their tale, the Romans were so impressed by the courage of the Zealots that they were unable to glory in their victory.

Sixty years later rebellion broke out again. In 131 CE an able Jewish leader called Simon Bar-Kokhba drove the Romans from Jerusalem and set up a new kingdom of Judea. This second Jewish revolt lasted for four years before the Roman armies regained the land, with massive slaughter of the ordinary people. Bar-Kokhba took refuge in the fortress of Beththether, southwest of Jerusalem, but eventually the Romans breached the walls, rushed in, and massacred the surviving defenders.

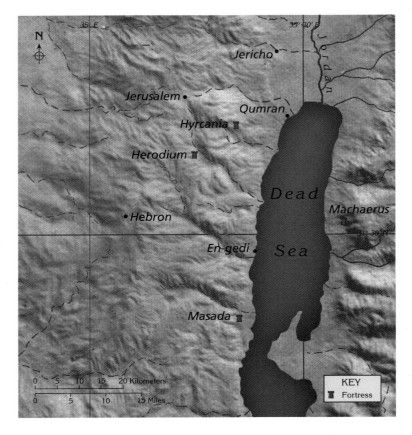

The Jewish Revolt, 70–73 CE
The map shows the location of Masada and other strongholds of the Jewish rebels in Judea during the final years of their first revolt. In 70 CE, Roman forces under Titus took Jerusalem. In 71-72 CE, the Romans destroyed the last centers of resistance, including the citadels of Herodium and Machaerus. The campaign ended with the siege and capture of Masada in 73 CE.

Northern Palace complex

Storerooms

Large bathhouse

Herod's private palace-villa

Palace complex with bathhouse

Zealots' living quarters

Herod's Palace-villa

N

Western Palace

Southern bastion

Groundplan of the fortress of Masada. Herod's great citadel was bounded by a powerful 'casemate' or double wall, which had 30 towers and four gates and contained 70 rooms. Within the citadel was a variety of buildings, including the Western Palace which combined administrative, residential, and ceremonial functions. To the north stood Herod's Northern Palace which included his private villa.

The large bathhouse in the Northern Palace included a caldarium, or hot room. The columns supported the floor, creating a space beneath – the hypocaust – through which hot air from a furnace circulated.

Aerial view of the remains of the Northern Palace complex at Masada. The three tiers of the palace-villa hang dramatically over a steep cliff. Above stand storerooms, administrative, buildings and a bathhouse.

Accommodation building

Western Palace

Zealots' living quarters

Mikve (ritual bath)

Double wall

Roman siege ramp

Synagogue

Herod's Palace

Middle level

Upper level

Lower level

The Fortress of Masada
Standing on a flat-topped rock towering above the Dead Sea, and surrounded on all sides by steep cliffs, Masada must have seemed impregnable to its Roman attackers. Water was supplied by a system of channels and aqueducts from nearby watercourses that fed 12 large cisterns. The Romans eventually breached Masada's defenses by using battering rams supported by a steep ramp that they constructed below the Western Palace.

Herod's Palace
In the main compound of the fortress at Masada stood Herod's large, official Western Palace and several smaller palaces for members of his family and important officials. But for his own use he built a palace-villa on three levels on the northern cliff face of the rock. Above the villa, on the Masada plateau, the palace complex included storerooms, administrative buildings, and the large bathhouse. The three tiers of the villa were connected to each other by staircases and contained magnificent frescoes – some on the lower level can still be seen today. The remains of Herod's own private bathhouse have also been discovered on this level. From this palace Herod would have had spectacular views out over the Dead Sea. By the time of the Zealots' occupation of Masada, the palace-villa lay derelict.

Marble statue of the emperor Domitian

The Book of Revelation, with its visionary emphasis and array of powerful images, is both the last and most mysterious book of the Bible. Even the identity of its author and the time of its writing are uncertain.

Naming himself simply as John, the author was probably not the Gospel writer of the same name, nor the disciple John, but possibly a Church elder from Asia Minor, sent as a convict or an exile to the island of Patmos in the Aegean. John is thought to have written Revelation during his time on the island, probably around 95 CE, in the reign of the Roman emperor Domitian. Revelation alludes to emperor worship and the persecution of the Christians, both of which were rife in this period. Others think that the book may date from an earlier time, perhaps from the reign of Nero, who persecuted the Christians in Rome in 64 CE.

The first three chapters of Revelation take the form of letters to seven churches in Asia Minor – encouraging them, upbraiding them, and warning them against immorality. The order of these letters suggests the route that might have been taken by a messenger delivering the book to the churches. From each of these centers the message could have been sent out to other Christian groups in the surrounding areas.

The Seven Churches of Asia
John addressed Revelation to 'the seven churches that are in Asia' – Ephesus, Smyrna, Pergamum, Thyatira, Sardis, Philadelphia, and Laodicea. Why he chose these particular churches, ignoring others set up by Paul, is not clear. The map below shows the eastern Mediterranean at the end of the 1st century CE and the possible route taken by a messenger delivering Revelation to these churches.

The Gate of Persecution *at Ephesus. John's first letter is addressed to the church in this city. He describes the church as flourishing but needing help to keep on the right track. Paul set up the church here during his third missionary journey.*

The Roman marketplace *in Smyrna (Izmir in modern Turkey) was a major center for emperor worship in Roman times. John's second letter was to the church here; he refers to the bitter persecution it suffers and sends encouragement.*

The Basilica of St John *at Pergamum, site of the third church written to by John. This basilica was once the Temple of Serapis but was converted during the Byzantine period. In John's time Pergamum was a famous center for medicine.*

The Altar of Zeus *was one of many temples and pagan shrines in Pergamum. John speaks of Satan's throne being at Pergamum and complains of false teachers and immoral practices within the city's Christian community.*

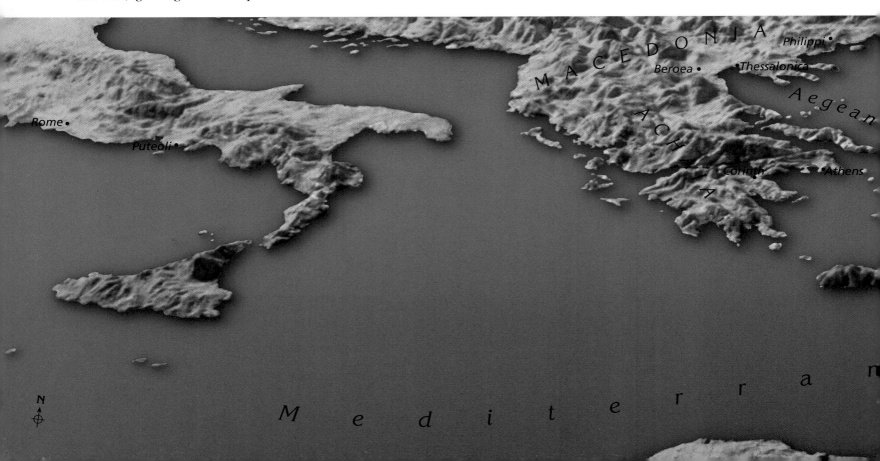

Rome

Puteoli

MACEDONIA   Philippi
Beroea   Thessalonica

Aegean

ACH

Corinth   Athens

Mediterran

N

The remaining 19 chapters of Revelation present a visionary account of the conflict between the forces of light and darkness, ending with the eventual destruction of 'Babylon' (representing Rome) and the triumph of God.

The book's imagery is difficult to interpret, especially for a modern reader, but much of its symbolism can be explained by reference to other parts of the Bible. The lamb, for instance, signifies Jesus Christ, who was associated with the sacrificial lamb of the Passover festival. Other symbols become clear in context, such as 'Babylon' meaning Rome.

Revelation bears similarities to Jewish 'apocalyptic' literature, mostly written between 170 BCE and 70 CE, a period when the Jews were subjugated by the Seleucids and the Romans. These texts aimed to give their readers hope that God would intervene to destroy their enemies. To avoid discovery and persecution for subversion, these writers used

Patmos is a small, rocky island off the southwestern coast of Asia Minor. John was exiled here, possibly as a convict to work in the mines, and he is thought to have written the Book of Revelation here. Pictured above is the courtyard of the island's Monastery of St John the Theologian.

a style laced with images and references recognizable only to their own people – a type of coded message.

This may account for some of Revelation's imagery – for instance, its symbolic use of the number 666, which is described as 'the number of the beast.' This could have been intended as a reference to Nero, for at this time letters were used to denote numbers, and the Hebrew letters for 'Emperor Nero' also represented the number 666. As a fierce persecutor of the Church, Nero would have been a fitting 'beast.'

Powerful though such symbolism is, these images are subservient to the major thrust of the narrative, which makes the book's ultimate message clear: God and the faithful will be the final victors in the conflict between good and evil.

The temple of Artemis at Sardis, now in ruins. The fifth church that John wrote to was located in Sardis – once the capital of the wealthy Lydian empire. John speaks bitingly of the Christians of the city as being complacent and 'dead.'

Philadelphia, site of John's sixth church, was a center for wine growing and the cult of the god Dionysus. The picture shows the remains of its city walls. The church here was weak, but it stood, John said, at the gate of great opportunity.

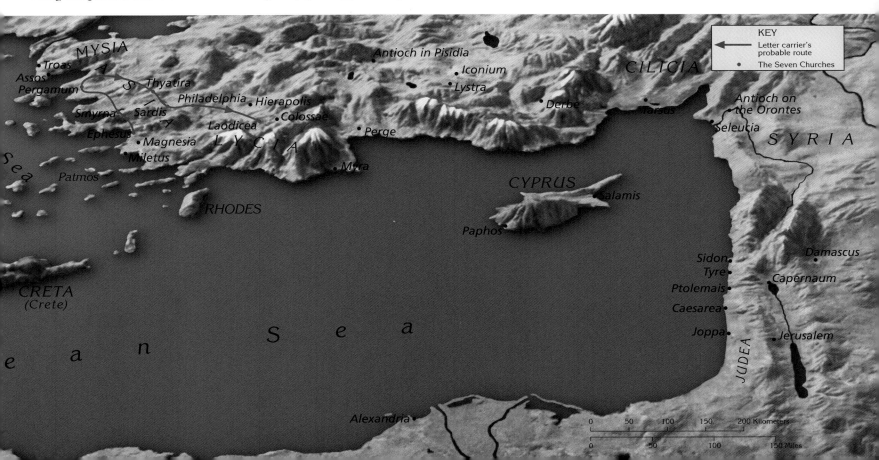

Acknowledgements

Brian Amos, Antonia Cunningham, Friedrich Naab, Palestine Exploration Fund, Patrick Mulrey, Philip Wilkinson.

Credits

Every effort has been made to trace the copyright holders of the illustrations used in this book. Any person or organisation having claims to ownership not identified above is invited to contact the publishers.

Abbreviations:
bottom *b*
centre *c*
left *l*
right *r*
top *t*

Page 1 AKG London; 2/3 Sonia Halliday Photographs; 4/5 AKG London *tl*, E T Archive *bl*; 6 Werner Neumeister *tl*, Zev Radovan *bl*, CM Dixon/Photo Resources *bc*; 6/7 Zev Radovan *bc*; 7 Zev Radovan *tl*, Sonia Halliday Photographs *tr*, *br*; 10 Zev Radovan *tl*, Thema *tc*, Corbis UK *br*; 11 Zev Radovan *br*; 12 Zev Radovan *tl*, *tr*, Thema *bl*; 12/13 E T Archive *c*; 13 S. Cohen/Stockmarket *tl*; 14 Zev Radovan *tl*, E T Archive *tc*; 15 Sonia Halliday Photographs *tc*, Zev Radovan *c*; 16 Thema *tl*, *bl*; 17 Thema *bc*, Christine Osborne/MEP *br*; 18/19 Erich Lessing/AKG London *background*; 18 inset pictures: Zev Radovan *tl*, Thema *cr*, Sonia Halliday Photographs *br*; 19 inset pictures: Sonia Halliday Photographs *cl*, AKG London *bl*, Zev Radovan *br*; 20 AKG London *tl*, Zev Radovan *tr*, E T Archive *br*; 21 Zev Radovan *br*; 22 Zev Radovan *tl*, Thema *bl*, AKG London *br*; 23 British Museum *cr*, Scala *b*; 24 Zev Radovan *tl*, E T Archive *tr*, Thema *b*; 25 Sonia Halliday Photographs *bc*, Zev Radovan *br*; 26 Zev Radovan *tl*, Thema *tr*,

Thema *bl*, Zev Radovan *br*; 27 Zev Radovan *br*; 28/29 Erich Lessing/AKG London *background*; 28 inset pictures: Zev Radovan *tl*, *c*, Panos Pictures *br*; 29 Zev Radovan *cr*, Panos Pictures *b*; 30 Thema *tl*, Sonia Halliday Photographs *tr*, *cr*, Jean-Loup Charmet *br*; 31 E T Archive *br*; 32 Zev Radovan *tl*, Sonia Halliday Photographs *tr*, *cr*; 33 E T Archive *cr*; 34 Zev Radovan *tl*, Thema *br*; 35 Thema *tl*, Zev Radovan *bc*; 36 Zev Radovan *tl*, *b*; 37 Zev Radovan *b*; 38/39 Marcello Bertinetti/Archivio White Star *background*; 38 inset pictures: Thema *t*, Zev Radovan *b*; 38/39 AKG London *c*, Zev Radovan *cr*, *br*; 40 Zev Radovan *tl*, *c*, *br*, Thema *tc*; 42 Zev Radovan *tl*; 42/43 Thema; 42 AV Foto Fasching Studio *b*; 43 Zev Radovan *tr*; 44 Zev Radovan *tl*; 44/45 E T Archive *bc*; 45 Sonia Halliday *tl*, Hulton-Getty Images *tr*; 46 Zev Radovan *tl*; 46/47 E T Archive *c*; 47 Zev Radovan *br*, Barry Seare/Sonia Halliday Photographs *bl*, Zev Radovan *cr*; 48/49 Zev Radovan; 50 Zev Radovan *tl*, *tr*, AV Foto Fasching Studio *br*, Zev Radovan *br*; 52 Zev Radovan *tl*, *cl*, AKG London *cr*; 54 Zev Radovan *tl*, Thema *tr*; 55 Zev Radovan *br*; 56/57 Zev Radovan *background*; 56 inset pictures: Thema *tl*, Zev Radovan *c*; 57 inset pictures: Zev Radovan *bc*, Thema *br*; 58 AKG London *tl*, *b*, *c*; 59 Thema *r*; 60 AKG London *tl*, Zev Radovan *c*, *b*; 61 Zev Radovan *tl*, Sonia Halliday Photographs *tr*; 62 Zev Radovan *tl*; 62/63 Zev Radovan *c*; 63 AKG London *tr*; 64 AKG London *tl*, Zev Radovan *tr*; 65 Zev Radovan *tl*, *tr*; 66/67 AKG London; 68 Zev Radovan *tl*, *tr*, Thema *tc*; 69 Sonia Halliday Photographs *tl*, *tc*, Christine Osborne/MEP *tr*; 70 Erwin Böhm *tl*, Zev Radovan *tr*, Christine Osborne/MEP *br*; 71 Zev Radovan *bl*, *br*; 72 Zev Radovan *tl*, Sonia Halliday Photographs *c*, AKG London *cr*; 73 Sonia Halliday Photographs *br*; 74 Zev Radovan *tl*, AKG London *bc*, E T Archive *br*; 74/75 Thema; 75 Zev

Radovan *br*; 76 Zev Radovan *tl*, *tr*; 77 Rijks Universiteit Leiden (Perizonius F17, f9v); 78/79 Zev Radovan; 80 Sonia Halliday Photographs *tl*, Zev Radovan *cl*, *cr*, Robert Harding Picture Library *c*, Thema *bc*; 81 AKG London; 82 Zev Radovan *tl*, Thema *tr*; 83 Christine Osborne/MEP; 84 Robert Harding Picture Library *tl*, Galaxy Picture Library *bl*; 84/85 Sonia Halliday Photographs; 85 Zev Radovan *tc*, *bl*, Hulton-Getty Images *tr*, Sonia Halliday Photographs *bc*; 86 Thema *tl*; 86/87 Sonia Halliday Photographs; 87 Zev Radovan *cl*, *c*, *bl*, *br*, AV Foto Fasching Studio *cr*, Katz/Mansell Collection *bc*; 88 Robert Harding Picture Library *tl*; 88/89 Sonia Halliday Photographs; 89 Zev Radovan *tr*, *c*, *bc*, *br*, Sonia Halliday Photographs *cr*; 90/91 Sonia Halliday Photographs *background*; 90 inset pictures: Sonia Halliday Photographs *tl*, Werner Neumeister *c*, Zev Radovan *b*; 91 Sonia Halliday Photographs *cr*, Zev Radovan *br*; 92 Zev Radovan *tl*, Werner Neumeister *tc*; 93 Sonia Halliday Photographs *tc*, Werner Neumeister *tr*, Zev Radovan *br*; 94 Zev Radovan *tl*, *bl*, Panos Pictures *bc*; 94/95 Sonia Halliday Photographs; 95 Robert Harding Picture Library *tl*, Zev Radovan *tc*, *tr*; 96/97 Robert Harding Picture Library *background*; 96 inset pictures: Scala/Museo di San Marco, Florence *cl*; 97 Thema *cr*, Christine Osborne/MEP *br*; 98 Zev Radovan *tl*, *cr*, Werner Neumeister *bl*; 98/99 Thema; 99 Sonia Halliday Photographs *tc*, *tr*; 100 Zev Radovan *tl*, *tr*; 101 Sonia Halliday Photographs *tc*, Zev Radovan *tr*; 102 Zev Radovan *tl*, Sonia Halliday Photographs *tr*; 102/103 Sonia Halliday Photographs; 103 Sonia Halliday Photographs; 104/105 Sonia Halliday Photographs 144*background*; 104 inset pictures: Robert Harding Picture Library *cl*, Sonia Halliday Photographs *bc*, *br*, Thema *cr*, Robert Harding Picture Library

br; 106 Zev Radovan; 107 Thema *tl*; 108 Sonia Halliday; 109 Zev Radovan *tl*, Werner Neumeister *tc*, *bcl*, *bcr*, *br*, Robert Harding Picture Library *tcr*, *bc*, Soni Halliday *tr*, *bl*; 110 Sonia Halliday Photographs *tl*, Zev Radovan *br*; 110/111 AKG London; 111 Sonia Halliday Photographs *cr*, Zev Radovan *br*; 112 Sonia Halliday Photographs *tl*, *c*; 112/113 Sonia Halliday Photographs; 113 E T Archive *tc*, Zev Radovan *cr*; 114 Zev Radovan *tl*, Sonia Halliday *tr*; 115 Sonia Halliday Photographs *t*, Zev Radovan *cr*, AKG London *bc*; 116 Robert Harding Picture Library *tl*, Sonia Halliday Photographs *bl*, *br*; 116/117 Bridgeman Art Library/Bibliothèque Nationale, Paris (Lat 1. f.386v); 118 E T Archive *tl*, CM Dixon/Photo Resources *tc*, Zev Radovan *c*, AKG London *cb*, Fotomas Index *bc*; 119 CM Dixon/Photo Resources *cl*, E T Archive *cr*; 120 AKG London *tl*; 120/121 Sonia Halliday Photographs; 121 Zev Radovan *tl*, *tr*, Sonia Halliday Photographs *cr*; 122 Zev Radovan *tl*, *br*, Sonia Halliday *bc*; 123 Zev Radovan *cl*, *br* Sonia Halliday *tl*; 124 Zev Radovan *tl*; 124/125 Sonia Halliday Photographs; 125 Sonia Halliday Photographs *c*, Zev Radovan *cr*; 126 Thema *tl*, *bl*, *bc*, Sonia Halliday Photographs *br*; 127 Thema; 128 Zev Radovan *tl*, *tr*; 128/129 E T Archive; 129 Zev Radovan *tc*, Sonia Halliday Photographs *tr*, E T Archive *br*; 130/131 Zev Radovan; 132/133 Erich Lessing/AKG London *background*; 132 inset pictures: Sonia Halliday Photographs *cl*, *c*, *br*, Zev Radovan *cr*, Christine Osborne/MEP *bc*; 134 Sonia Halliday Photographs; 135 Sonia Halliday *tl*, Thema *tc*, *tr*; 136 Zev Radovan *tl*; 136/137 Erich Lessing/AKG London; 137 Zev Radovan *br*; 138 Zev Radovan; 139 Zev Radovan *tc*, Sonia Halliday *tr*; 140 AKG London *tl*, Sonia Halliday Photographs *tc*, *tr*, *c*, *cr*; 141 Sonia Halliday Photographs.